Studying Drama

Studying Drama

An Introduction

MALCOLM KELSALL
Professor of English Literature,
University College Cardiff

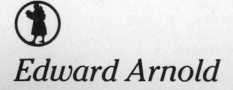

Edward Arnold

© Malcolm Kelsall 1985

First published in Great Britain 1985 by
Edward Arnold (Publishers) Ltd,
41 Bedford Square, London WC1B 3DQ

Edward Arnold (Australia) Pty Ltd,
80 Waverley Road, Caulfield East,
Victoria 3145, Australia

British Library Cataloguing in Publication Data

Kelsall, Malcolm
  Studying drama : an introduction.
  1. Drama
  I. Title
  809.2   PN1655

  ISBN 0–7131–6450–6

Text set in 10/11pt Cheltenham Book Compugraphic
by Colset Private Limited, Singapore
Printed and bound in Great Britain by
Richard Clay (The Chaucer Press) Ltd, Bungay, Suffolk

Contents

Acknowledgements

The publishers would like to thank the following for permission to include copyright material: Faber and Faber Publishers, London and Grove Press Inc., New York for extracts from Samuel Beckett: *Krapp's Last Tape* (© 1957 by Samuel Beckett; copyright 1958, 1959, 1960 by Grove Press Inc.) and Tom Stoppard: *Rosencrantz and Guildenstern are Dead* (© 1967 by Tom Stoppard); and Macmillan Publishers Ltd, London and Basingstoke for extracts from Sean O'Casey: *Juno and the Paycock*.

1 Action

Just as a wheelwright makes wheels, a playwright makes plays. The work is a craft. The discussion which follows concerns plays as theatrecraft. In what way can the reader better understand the written text as theatre? Without the craft there is nothing. A wheel which falls to pieces on the road is a bad wheel; a piece of theatre which will not play is bad theatre.

Since plays are written for performance they are different in their nature from novels or poetry. Reading Wordsworth's *The Prelude* is a private and individual act. One is alone with the text in silence and in solitude. Perhaps reading aloud will more clearly reveal the shape of the verse rhythms: many poems and novels have been dramatically read before audiences. However, public performance is not an essential part of their nature. But *Hamlet* was written so that the lines might be spoken by actors in a public theatre, and it is shaped with the conventions of that kind of theatre in mind. Parts of the play do not exist as 'literature' at all, but only as stage directions. The play within a play is preceded by a dumb show. We see the murder of a king, but we hear nothing. That silence is as expressive as words. In it, like Hamlet, we watch for the reaction of Claudius to the murder. But he says nothing, at that time.

To learn to read a play is to learn to understand its potential as theatre. Not to see that potential is to impoverish the text. Of course, it can be read other ways: grammatically, philosophically, sociologically – or even prop up a table leg. But a play cannot be read just as if it were a novel or a poem. But I write *read* not *perform*. This discussion is not a manual for performers. Indeed performance is not necessarily a help. The school trip to see a bad production of a classic text can even be a hindrance. It is painful to watch ignorance hand in hand with incompetence. Even good performance is only a partial aid.

1

We learn something of what can be done with a text in the theatre, but what we see and hear is only part of a vast ocean of potential. The choices that have been made of necessity exclude other choices each, perhaps, equally valid and exciting.

Something may be learnt from the attempt to perform, especially from the discipline of direction and the close study of words as spoken and of movement. But the imperfect nature of untrained technique is a handicap, and the very mechanics of performance can interfere with a deeper understanding of the playwright's craft: do I come in left or right? have I learnt the right cue? help! props have forgotten to give me the letter I must deliver! Such experience is of limited utility. But the first thing apparent in putting together any performance is that everyone starts with a book or manuscript in their hands. One begins by reading, and until one has learnt to read the text theatrically, nothing will be properly effected.

The text, then, is a provocative to performance, or the shadow cast by performance. It was Aristotle who wrote of plays as being an imitation of an action, and it is that sense of action – words in movement, bodies in movement – that is the first thing to be grasped. It is the essence of theatre, and which the text least effectively represents. Let us take an example – one that may be a little disturbing. (This short book proceeds by example.) Consider the last scene of a recent popular success at the Mermaid Theatre. Claire Luckham's *Trafford Tanzi*. It will not be quoted for there are, in the main, no words for the principal performers to speak. The action takes place in a wrestling ring, and the protagonists are fighting. The printed text is primarily detailed instructions for that fight. The atmosphere created was that of a popular wrestling match – the kind of thing to be seen any Saturday afternoon on television. The use of theatre for this kind of show would not have surprised the Elizabethans. The playhouse was an entertainment centre. The audience who first saw the wrestling match in *As You Like It*, or the fencing match in *Hamlet*, would judge with the same experienced eye for skill as a modern audience at *Trafford Tanzi*.

The fight is long, hard and professional. The audience, men and women, shout encouragement, abuse, ribaldry, obscenity – providing an improvised dialogue. The fight is unusual in one respect. It is between a man and a woman. The winner will go out and pursue a career, the loser will look after the home.

The man expects to win. He is arrogant. But the woman is the better fighter. The man is exhausted, sexually humiliated, defeated.

This simple example contains many of the essential elements of theatre. The action upon stage is built from the relationship between the players: husband and wife; antagonists in a fight. Neither could perform alone. What is done provokes response: action and reaction. Here it is conflict, like Hamlet against Laertes. Paradoxically that conflict also rests upon co-operation, for unless the action and reaction were structured the performance would not achieve its predetermined end: Tanzi might have her arm really broken, Hamlet might lose an eye. The creation of a living relation between players to achieve a certain end is the essence of theatre. In this it is analogous to circus – the trapeze artists' art – or even a football match. In *literary* theatre with which we are concerned – plays as things written – even monologue concerns other people. No one was born in isolation or grows up in a vacuum, and although it is possible to conceive exceptions (Samuel Beckett has experimented with minimal theatre, as we shall see), the normal condition of all theatre concerns human relationship. If this is so, if plays concern the action and reaction of players within a structured framework, then the traditional demand 'write a character study of Hamlet' can be seriously misleading. It asks for the isolation of something which exists only as relationships.

The audience in *Trafford Tanzi* have a necessary part to play. Their impromptu comments and reactions are part of the entertainment. The action between the players would have no purpose if it did not provoke reaction from the spectators (likewise circus). Theatre is a public act which depends upon an audience, and which is even conditioned by it – laughter in comedy is infectious and part of the collective experience. That is why television comedy introduces laughter into its programmes. In other kinds of theatre audience and actors sometimes even mingle. At the end of court masque in the seventeenth century – a formal entertainment with elaborate allegorical scenes and complex dances with moral meaning – the players might quit the stage for the auditorium at the end and actors and audience join together in another dance (signifying social harmony and concord). In *Trafford Tanzi* the gentleman who took off his jacket (it is reported) and tried to climb into the ring to fight the triumphant woman was, in a way, parodying a seventeenth-century custom (signifying social disharmony!). This essential public relationship of theatrical performance has often led to the suggestion that plays are a form of ritual. That is a very lofty claim. It is certainly true that they seek to speak or show matters of social concern. Tanzi's victory makes obvious claims about woman's role in contemporary Britain.

Consider next another action concerning the relation of men and women. The episode is from Middleton and Rowley's *The Changeling* (1624). Beatrice is to be married by her father Vermandero to Alonzo against her will for she loves Alsemero. Meantime she is pursued by the ugly serving man De Flores. (Later she will hire De Flores to murder Alonzo, and as the price, has to become his mistress.) We do not know the audience reaction to this play, but we do know that a few years later the Puritan revolutionaries closed the playhouses as immoral places. The conclusion of this scene may partly show why.

There are two problems in the action which the student is invited to solve. The text, as printed, lacks all stage directions (except for one *Exeunt*). Certain significant actions occur, however. Beatrice drops a glove, and it is picked up. When, and by whom? Some lines are spoken between the actors, others to the audience (aside, or in monologue). Which are which? Modern editions, of course, sort these things out. When these matters are resolved the significance of the action may be discussed. Vermandero is speaking to Alsemero of Alonzo.

Vermandero	I would not change him for a son-in-law For any he in Spain, the proudest he, And we have great ones, that you know.
Alsemero	He's much Bound to you, sir.
Vermandero	He shall be bound to me, As fast as this tie can hold him; I'll want My will else.
Beatrice	I shall want mine if you do it.
Vermandero	But come, by the way I'll tell you more of him.
Alsemero	How shall I dare to venture in his castle, When he discharges murderers at the gate?

	But I must on, for back I cannot go.
Beatrice	Not this serpent gone yet?
Vermandero	Look, girl, thy glove's fall'n.
	Stay, stay, – De Flores help a little.
De Flores	Here, lady.
Beatrice	Mischief on your officious forwardness!
	Who bade you stoop? They touch my hand no more:
	There, for t'other's sake I part with this,
	Take 'em and draw thine own skin off with 'em.

Exeunt

De Flores	Here's favour come, with a mischief! Now I know
	She had rather wear my pelt tann'd in a pair
	Of dancing pumps, than I should thrust my fingers
	Into her sockets here, I know she hates me,
	Yet cannot choose but love her. . . . (I.i.215–35)

Probably the glove is dropped on the line 'Not this serpent gone yet', which is one of the numerous asides. Where is the glove dropped, why is it dropped, and what is the significance of the action? Possibly it is merely an accident. That is her father's interpretation – or perhaps what he publically wishes to declare – for another possibility is that the glove is a lover's token; she drops it so that by the action she can say to Alsemero what she cannot say in words: she loves him not Alonzo. It is her intention that he should pick it up, and that it should be a cause for establishing a relation between them, even a gift such as a lady might give to a knight at a tournament.

But it is De Flores who picks it up, leading to the extraordinary exaggeration of her reaction in giving to him both garments which then he uses, after her departure, as a sexual symbol when he thrusts his fingers in. (Later, when De Flores kills Alonzo, he brings Beatrice one of the dead man's fingers as a token that the deed is done.) Is it possible, then, that the glove is dropped not *for* Alsemero, but *because* of De Flores? He is closer to her than Alsemero. That aside 'Not this serpent gone yet' can only refer to De Flores (and as the serpent who tempted Eve). In her alarm she drops the glove 'accidentally', but in fact it is a token that informs the audience that she will give herself to De Flores, and thus, to underline the commitment to the murderer who will deflower her, she gives him the second glove also. A Freudian reading of the action would be that she is, unconsciously, even now more attracted by the ugly, evil man than by Alsemero.

Or is the dropping of the glove like the throwing down of a gauntlet before a combat – who will pick it up? Consider the position of the isolated woman in a male society – a position emphasized by her isolation in the action upon the stage. Every man wants her; her father will dispose of her. She is the subject of intolerable pressures which cannot be voiced. The asides draw the audience into the predicament of the players who cannot speak among themselves what they really feel. The harmony which appears on the surface conceals great rifts underneath. The woman cannot act directly. A man must act for her. If she throws down her glove – who is so bold as to pick it up?

The when and the how of the action, the way the glove is picked up, the drawing off of the second garment, the intrusion of the fingers into the sockets, and the continual, unvoiced, physical inter-relationship between the players – these are elements of the scene of prime importance, and inseparable from interpretation of the dialogue. Moreover, the audience are not merely spectators of the scene. The asides are appeals to their understanding. The events demand interpretation, and that interpretation has many levels and possibilities. The range of potentiality, and the complex inter-relation of action and dialogue in this episode make this a richer piece of theatrecraft than our original example.

Consider now a longer sequence. The illustration is from *The Playboy of the Western World* (1907) by J.M. Synge. The action concerns young Christy Mahon who seeks shelter in a low drinking house in remote Mayo. He tells a story how he killed his father with a blow from a potato spade because his father wanted him to marry an old woman. The daughter of the house, Pegeen, is fascinated by the tale, and falls in love with Christy whose confidence grows as their love develops. He becomes a local hero, and Pegeen throws over her cowardly fiancé, the religious Shawn Keogh. But then Christy's father arrives – with merely a bloody bandage round his head. To recover his reputation Christy hits him again (off stage) and appears to have really killed him. But now the villagers, alarmed for their safety, turn on Christy. There is a 'great gap', Pegeen says, between a splendid story and a 'dirty deed'. A rope is dropped over Christy's head.

He is pulled down on the floor

Christy   (*twisting his legs round the table*) Cut the rope, Pegeen, and I'll quit the lot of you, and live from this out, like the madmen of Keel, eating muck and green weeds, on the faces of the cliffs.

Pegeen   And leave us to hang, is it, for a raving liar, the like of you? (*To* Men) Take him on, out from this.

Shawn   Pull a twist on his neck, and squeeze him so.

Philly   Twist yourself. Sure he cannot hurt you, if you keep your distance from his teeth alone.

Shawn   I'm afeard of him. (*To* Pegeen) Lift a lighted sod, will you, and scorch his leg.

Pegeen   (*blowing the fire with a bellows*) Leave go now, young fellow, or I'll scorch your shins.

Christy   You're blowing for to torture me? That's your kind, is it? Then let the lot of you be wary, for, if I've to face the gallows, I'll have a gay march down, I tell you, and shed the blood of some of you before I die.

Shawn   Keep a good hold, Philly. Be wary, for the love of God. For I'm thinking he would liefest wreak his pains on me.

Christy   If I do lay my hands on you, it's the way you'll be at the fall of night, hanging as a scarecrow for the fowls of hell. Ah, you'll have a gallous jaunt I'm saying, coaching out through Limbo with my father's ghost.

Shawn   (*to* Pegeen) Make haste, will you? Oh, isn't he a holy terror, and isn't it true for Father Reilly, that all drink's a curse that has the lot of you so shaky and uncertain now?

Christy   If I can wring a neck among you, I'll have a royal judgment looking on the trembling jury in the courts of law. . . *He squirms round on the floor and bites* Shawn's *leg.*

Shawn   My leg's bit on me! He's the like of a mad dog, I'm thinking, the way that I will surely die.

Christy   You will then, the way you can shake out hell's flags of welcome for my coming in two weeks or three, for I'm thinking Satan hasn't many have killed their da in Kerry and in Mayo too.

Old Mahon *comes in behind on all fours and looks on unnoticed*

Men   (*to* Pegeen) Bring the sod, will you.

Pegeen   (*coming over*) Gold help him so.   (*Burns his leg*)

Christy   (*kicking and screaming*) Oh, glory be to God!

Jimmy   (*seeing* Old Mahon) Will you look what's come in?

                                    They all drop Christy *and run left*

Christy   (*scrambling on his knees face to face with* Old Mahon) Are
           you coming to be killed a third time, or what ails you now?

                                                                   (Act III)

This scene has general analogies with the end of *Trafford Tanzi*. In it the woman has physical mastery over the man, and the vital action centres upon their relationship. It comes from a play which we know, as a matter of history, was substantially affected by its audience. *The Playboy* provoked riots in the theatre during the week of its first run, and was performed, often inaudibly, under police protection. It was viewed as an obscene insult to the Irish people (an equivalent perhaps of playing *The Merchant of Venice* or *The Jew of Malta* in Jerusalem). As a result substantial alterations were made in the text, and the peasants, gradually, prettified. Now, in the passage of time, these problems are anaesthetized.

But the nature of the action remains problematical. In what way is Christy Mahon tied up; how is Shawn bitten; how does Pegeen Mike burn him with the sod? The stage directions tell us these things must be done, but they do not tell us how, and unless we know, the signification of the scene is indefinable. Put in bald terms, is this text a piece of farce, or tragedy?

Strenuous physical action in a comic framework is often farcical, and physical punishment in farce is not felt as particularly painful – the slapstick of circus clowns is a clear example, or, in Ben Jonson's comedy *The Alchemist* a blindfold character is pinched and tormented by confidence tricksters pretending to be fairies, and audiences laugh. The binding of Christy is shortly followed by the extraordinary climax of Old Mahon's entry on hands and knees, his confrontation with his son, and the line 'Are you coming to be killed a third time, or what ails you now?' If that is funny, then it suggests that the audience do not feel the binding, the biting, or the burning with the sod as particularly painful or cruel (compare a torture scene in Renaissance drama) and that Christy is surprised rather than hurt by his fall from favour in Pegeen's eyes.

Alternatively the scene is tragic. We thought we were watching a comedy (albeit an odd sort of comedy) but suddenly our own experience becomes that of the peasant community, what was story becomes 'real'. The tying up is the frightened and vicious act of a community seeking out a scapegoat, and we are intended to feel the pain of that burning sod which is pressed against Christy to hurt, and which makes him scream.

These alternatives are put as extremes. It need not be divided so clearly. Some of the characters may remain in the comic world, while others (especially Pegeen) have entered tragic theatre. Such mixture of genres is not uncommon. The porter scene in *Macbeth*, the clown at Cleopatra's death in *Antony and Cleopatra*, the conclusion of Marlowe's *The Jew of Malta* (to be discussed later), are good examples of such blending.

But Synge's text does not instruct the reader, or the actor: play this as farce, this as tragedy. The action is open to variety of interpretation. There is potential here the outer limits of which can be described, but those limits are very wide indeed – farce/tragedy – and hence the variation between them is very great. Nor will performance 'solve' the 'problem'. An intelligent director and cast may well wish to explore various ways of playing the scene, and the way in which the part is examined will depend upon how they view the whole (especially, how does the action resolve itself after this scene?). They will settle what is best for them in that production. The potentiality of the action remains.

The action of the players in this scene is an important determinant on how one interprets the roles. It has already been suggested that the demand 'write a character study of Hamlet' asks one to separate the inseparable. Let us consider the character of Pegeen in this sequence. It is apparent that what is written for her to say tells very little about how she performs her crucial action – burning her lover – and even less about why the act is performed, or what she might think and feel. But before one even speculates about the inner, the invisible self of Pegeen, one must ask is Pegeen a character in a farce, a comedy, or a tragedy, because how she acts depends upon what sort of role she has.

This is fundamental. In Marjorie Boulton's *The Anatomy of Drama* there is an extraordinary passage in which she asks how Olivia in *Twelfth Night* 'a lady of wealth, position, refinement and sensitivity, marries a man she hardly knows, in eager haste, and is not distressed when she finds she has accidentally married the brother of the man who first took her fancy and who was a girl in disguise' and provides psychological justification for the marriage. Poppycock. Characters in romantic comedies do not perform like characters in real life. Likewise even in remotest Mayo sons do not repeatedly hit their father on the head with potato spades, and become heroes by telling their tale. Whatever the relation of play to truth, it is not that. Therefore the manner in which Pegeen performs her speechless action of bringing the sod from the fire is not determined by the fact that this is a true story, it is performed, rather, in the way appropriate to the kind of play in which her role is conceived, just as, when Papageno in the comedy *The Magic Flute* decides to hang himself (because he cannot obtain the wife he wants) he does not go about his task in the same way as Othello killing himself because Desdemona is dead. Characters in comedies do not behave like characters in tragedies.

Nor is Pegeen's silence before the fire ultimately penetrable. Appeal to performance, again, does not 'solve' the 'problem'. One might argue that an accomplished actress, by the way she moves, by the expression on her face, by the tone of voice in which she speaks her lines will tell us what is happening which is not written in the text. I would not wish to deny the immense expressive power of embodied action. But actors are not semaphors signalling everything. Let us assume, for a moment, that Pegeen's role is tragic. She has seen the disastrous nature of her lot. She had given her love and faith to a storyteller who is not the hero of her imagination – but there is nothing worthwhile remaining in the community around her. (She is to end the play in 'wild lamentation' – the keen, a mourning song for the dead.) Granted that, can the act express all the thoughts and emotions which might be in that mind, were she a real person: love, hate, disappointed hope and imagination, self-punishment, shame, outrage? – does the list need to be extended? – this is perhaps even a ritual act, a symbolic gesture separating herself from Christy by a formal and public token of rejection. All that may be hypothesized – but ultimately what the text gives us is Pegeen's silence while she prepares the sod, and an action manifold in the way it can be performed. What one must recognize is the potentiality of silence to suggest. It is not to be explained away.

There remains another possibility in the action we see. It cannot be approached without quoting the words that are spoken and therefore marks the kind of limit one reaches in the conception of play simply as action. The laying on of the sod is accompanied by an appeal to God, Pegeen's 'God help him so', Christy's 'Glory be to God!'. One suggested possibility in the action has been that this is a ritual gesture by Pegeen. Supposing that ritual is religious? The action upon stage, the picture which we see, is made to carry a religious, or moral signification. It is therefore an icon (an image carrying religious signification) or an emblem (a visible representation of an abstract idea). In the Christian religion the demons in hell often carry burning spits with which they torture the damned for their sins. Does Pegeen represent retributive Christian justice at this moment, and Christy one who has yielded to the power of Satanism (our information, at this juncture, is that he has just killed his father)?. If this is so, the emphasis of the scene may be upon the formal message to be communicated, and upon the burning as a ritual act, rather than upon naturalistic causation: what makes a woman behave to her lover this way? Given that reading, one begins to question the very name of the tormented character: Christy. Drop the 'y' and he becomes a Christ figure.

It is impossible to make any worthwhile assessment of the potential validity of this latter reading of the action without the wider context of the play as a whole. (This is so, of course, more or less for all extracts.) One might ask does the play possess an extended series of Christian allusions, does the dramatist work by using such formal devices elsewhere? It would be appropriate to ask something of the audience – is it relevant that this play was written in a Roman Catholic community? – and of the dramatist – is it significant that Synge frequently assaults the sensibilities of the community in which he works (hence the riots which greeted the play)? If there were no supportive evidence it would be reasonable to conclude that since *The Playboy* is not a work which uses Christian images elsewhere, it would be unlikely that there were such an abrupt change here. On the other hand, if the evidence were positive, the probability of an emblematic interpretation of the action would be greater. The potential of the episode increases.

A number of questions have been put about this text, and not answered. Is that uncomfortable? It is pleasant to rely upon the certainties of assured instruction: this is the meaning of the text, and here are the reasons why it means this. But literature is not like that, and theatre texts least of all because they are provocatives to action, and that action is variable. Plays are not like Latin grammar or geometry. That is why English litera-ture is a difficult subject. There are often no correct solutions.

The does not mean that anything goes. It is possible to envis-age an interpretation of the extract from *The Playboy* which argues that the passage shows the influence of English colonial oppression upon an exploited people who are corrupted by their situation into internal violence whereas if they were properly trained in Marxist dialectic they would direct their energies to destroying their class oppressors and establishing a socialist state by expropriating the land for themselves. (David Hare's Marxist Chinese peasants in *Fanshen* might be com-pared with Synge's Irish peasants in *The Playboy*.) Interpreta-tions of this kind are not uncommon in English literary critic-ism. But can such a reading be made to stand up in relation to the text of the extract? One might criticize Synge for not being a Marxist, but that is another thing.

This raises the question of ideology, however, which, like character, is an issue for discussion in a separate chapter. The purpose of this introduction has been merely to emphasize the fundamental nature of the action – the play is written to be performed – and to indicate that the dialogue is not always the most important guide to significant actions. What occurs in silence can be more emphatic than what is said. That is an easy concept.

What is difficult is that the action has a range of potential, and the bounds of that potential may be very wide indeed. All one can do is look at the text in the way Launcelot Brown looked at landscape: it has 'capabilities' he used to say. A bit of common sense is always a good thing. Brown would not try to turn a bog into a mountain, though he could see how a stream might become a lake. But if one studies the reception of texts it soon becomes apparent how wide the capabilities are. *The Playboy* was seen as an obscene libel; *Richard II* was used by Essex to try to start a revolution. Probably those who turned up at the Abbey Theatre in 1907 to shout down the play before they heard it were not in the best frame of mind to study theatre. They lacked scholarly objectivity. They were not there to ask 'what is truth?' – even less to ask is this a comedy, or a tragedy? – but to use the text as a trampoline on which to bounce their own political views. But, then, theatre is not a scholarly, objective mode of enquiry after truth. It moves audiences to laughter, tears, stimulates thought, arouses anger, disturbs. That is one reason why *Trafford Tanzi* is here. The contemporary subject touches our sexuality. As for scholarly objectivity, and truth – if they are desirable ideals (and not everyone agrees that they are), can we be assured we possess them? An engineer once said, 'Give me a fulcrum and I will move the world' – but where is that fulcrum to be placed?

Perhaps we can be more confident with the play as craftsmanship – which is where we began. We can tell how a wheelwright makes wheels, a potter casts pots, how Rembrandt applied paint. Technique can be described, and technique is the basis of everything. But the questions of interpretation will not stay away. What does it mean? In what way does it come home to me? How have others seen it? Am I asking the right questions? What others might I ask? If this line of thought were followed through, what might the consequences be? One shapes the matter this way, and then that. Is this chapter itself the right way to begin? Do the arguments make sense? That is what studying is about. Welcome to the debate.

2 The Empty Space

A theatre is any space in which actors and audience are brought into relation. The making of a stage creates special significance. The eye reads the stage as if it were a book. It asks 'what is the meaning of the objects within that space?' The emotions as well as the intelligence may be moved. Expectation is aroused. A space hung with heavy drapes in red and black may declare: this is a tragedy which will be performed. A fantasy painted Gothic castle sparkling with gold and silver dust may suggest fairy tale, romance, pantomime. The whole theatre itself may create an effect. A recent production of *The Playboy of the Western World* was moved from the Lyttelton auditorium to the Olivier at the National Theatre. The scene – the interior of a small peasant pub – was seen in the Lyttelton filling the space within the proscenium arch: the audience were intimately related to the actors, sharing, as it were, the same room with them. The emphasis was upon domestic comedy. In the large spaces of the Olivier the cottage was a tiny lit place in a large area of surrounding half light. The scene suggested the loneliness of remote Mayo, and a larger dimension to the action. The poetic, the tragic potential of the text was heightened.

So too, within the set, costume and make-up speak their own special language: Harlequin and Columbine are not dressed like King Lear and Cordelia; the ugly sisters in *Cinderella* do not look like Goneril and Reagan. Lighting, music, sound play their part in creating the scene. How frequently Shakespeare uses music! Sometimes other senses are evoked. In a recent production of Strindberg's tragedy *Miss Julie* the audience smelt breakfast cooking. It is a naturalistic play. The odour of bacon frying heightened the sense of the real.

Plays are often written for particular stages, even specific companies. We know more about some than about others. The histories of the Abbey Theatre and the Royal Court in our own century are well documented; concerning the classic Greek theatre we know little more than can be seen by standing in the ruins. Particularly tantalizing for the English stage is a half knowledge of the theatres of Shakespeare's London. Some sense is useful of the history of the stage on which plays were performed, how the players were dressed, how they looked, but one must recognize too that plays are not prisoners of their history. Their potential renews itself through change.

Illustration is easier for the modern stage than for earlier time. Few early theatres survive, and none for Shakespeare's time, unless we count the great halls of the houses of the age where travelling players performed, or the yards of ancient coaching inns. For some of us Victorian or Edwardian theatres are our earliest knowledge of the nature of acting space. The dramatists of the nineteenth century onwards have left frequent detailed descriptions of the nature of the set, properties, costume required for production. Before that the briefest reference might often suffice: 'Valentine in his Chamber Reading. Jeremy writing. Several books upon the Table'; 'A Room in Foresight's House' – that is all Congreve tells us of the setting for the first two acts of the Restoration comedy *Love for Love*. Before that the instructions 'Enter', 'Exit', 'Exeunt' might be all that is recorded.

Here is the description of the setting for Sean O'Casey's *Juno and the Paycock*:

The living-room of a two-room tenancy occupied by the Boyle family in a tenement house in Dublin. Left, a door leading to another part of the house; left of door a window looking into the street; at back a dresser; farther to right at back, a window looking into the back of the house. Between the window and the dresser is a picture of the Virgin; below the picture, on a bracket, is a crimson bowl in which a floating votive light is burning. Farther to the right is a small bed partly concealed by cretonne hangings strung on a twine. To the right is the fireplace; near the fireplace is a door leading to the other room. Beside the fireplace is a box containing coal. On the mantleshelf is an alarm clock lying on its face. In a corner near the window looking into the back is a galvanized bath. A table and some chairs. On the table are breakfast things for one. A teapot is on the hob and a frying-pan stands inside the fender. There are a few books on the dresser and one on the table. Leaning against the dresser is a long-handled shovel – the kind invariably used by labourers when turning concrete or mixing mortar. Johnny Boyle is sitting crouched beside the fire. Mary with her jumper off – it is lying on the back of a chair – is arranging her hair before a tiny mirror perched on the table.

The play was first performed at the Abbey Theatre, Dublin in 1924 on a stage within a proscenium arch. The date of the action of the play is 1922. It was, therefore, a contemporary setting. It is a play about Dublin performed in Dublin. The audience are expected to recognize a room such as might be found if they went round the corner and entered a tenement house.

O'Casey expects that recognition when he writes of 'a two-room tenancy'. What the audience actually see are two doors leading out of one room. The subsequent action will define the nature and function of the doors, one leading into the only bedroom possessed by a family whose two grown up children are seen on stage, the other leading *not* into the outer world directly, but into the tenement house of which this is a tenancy. Through that door other members of the community who live in the tenement will come and go. One thing this may suggest is the lack of privacy of the poor: 'In a corner near the window looking into the back is a galvanized bath.' That bath is never used in the play. Its function is to suggest the other kinds of action which might occur in this room. Likewise 'Farther to the right is a small bed partly concealed by cretonne hangings strung on a twine.' The bed is often employed, most usually by Johnny who has been crippled fighting against the British, also as a hiding place by Mrs Boyle. It too tells one more of the nature of life of the poor. If that is Johnny's bed, where is Mary's in this two-room tenement? We see her in her under-clothes (a little shocking in 1922) putting on make-up at the kitchen table. As for the parents, Juno and 'Captain' Boyle, what of their life together? The action of the play will show how little is left in the marriage, which Juno holds together by hard work for the sake of the family. Nothing explicit is said about marital intimacy. O'Casey does not need to. The set tells us.

The windows will have their function. The one that looks into the street leads into the outer world through which tragedy will come. Through it the Captain will see the gunman knocking at the street door. He brings a summons to death for Johnny. Through the same window the family see the funeral of Mrs Tancred's son, who has been killed in the Irish civil war. The other window, to the back, is used for the comic world of the play. The lay-about Joxer, the Captain's side-kick, climbs out of it to hide from Juno – through it he makes a farcical appearance at an inappropriate moment when we have all but forgotten that he is still out there. By the end of the play those windows are associated in the minds of the audience with two different kinds of story, and two different kinds of theatre: the tragic and the comic.

The various properties which O'Casey lists each have a particular piece of information to convey, and a dramatic function to perform. The picture of the Virgin Mary and the votive light indicate that this is a Roman Catholic household. Before Johnny's death, the light suddenly goes out, and remains extinguished until the end of the play. The fire and the coal speak of the domestic hearth as the centre of the family; they also tell that the Boyles cook and eat where they sit and live. Breakfast will be eaten where Mary is making up and reading the paper. The long-handled shovel tells us that someone in this house is a navvy. In fact the shovel becomes a comic property, because Captain Boyle is too lazy to work – that is one reason why the alarm clock is face downward. The other man of the household, who could use the shovel, Johnny, is a cripple. The workers in this house are the women. The books which are scattered about are not what one would necessarily expect. Mary is discovered reading, and the association of reading and books we might thus make with her, is correct. She has intellectual aspirations to escape from the slum. Some of the books are identified later. They are by the daring new dramatist Ibsen. One of them is *A Doll's House* which concerns a woman's attempt to escape from her environment. Mary, we shall learn, throws over her lover, Jerry, a labourer, for the upwardly mobile schoolteacher Charles Bentham. This leads to her tragedy.

Almost everything O'Casey mentions, therefore, carries information. Some of it one gets at once. Other matters are subject to delay before they acquire their signification. Another matter of great substance has not yet been discussed, however. We are told this is 'a tenement house in Dublin'.

O'Casey did not describe what he meant by that, because his audience knew, and his set designer and stage crew constructed a box set from immediate knowledge. This room has been a grand Georgian room. The doors may show signs of pediments, the ceilings cornices, the windows are large sash casements. This naturalistic detail derives from historical fact – the slum dwellers in Dublin had moved in on a once smart Georgian area of town – but it carries a message about the pretensions of Ireland herself. The set juxtaposes grandeur and squalor. The Boyle family, in their aspirations (and by means of the money they inherit during the play) have grand designs, which are checked by low realities. Ireland, in her national aspirations, uses a grandiloquent rhetoric. The facts are that young men die brutally, and without apparent benefit to anyone. At the end of the play O'Casey removes all the furniture and properties from this set, so the room alone is left to make a statement about the home that is removed from it.

If we were to move a step further, from reading theatrically to planning production, it would also become apparent how much O'Casey has omitted in his description, and yet which it is crucial to supply correctly. He mentions a dresser, but he does not state what is on it. The fireplace has a mantelshelf. What is on it besides the alarm clock? This is the kind of naturalistic play which invites speculation about the life of the characters outside the action of the piece – hence the galvanized bath. What kind of people are they, what kind of lives do they lead when not in this action? To complete dressing the set is not merely an exercise in historical accuracy – the pieces must be in period – it is a continuation of the expressive information which O'Casey has already given one. What kind of crockery does Juno put on her dresser? Will that, as far as poverty permits, show some upward desire? Is she neat, or a sloven? Are there family photographs upon the mantelshelf? If so, of what kind? Mary at confirmation? A wedding group? How do the Boyles light the fire, or cigarettes or a pipe? With matches, or spills or paper? If spills, what sort of spills? All this, in reading, can only be peripheral. But the set tells one it is the kind of play where such kind of questions are relevant, and, indeed, in production must be indicated. This is intrinsic to naturalistic theatre. It invites us to forget that the stage is a stage.

Even within this naturalistic mode we are, of course, always aware we are in a theatre. The front window belongs to tragedy, the back window to comedy. The Georgian room has an expressive function which is akin to a poetic metaphor. It comments upon the action, and enlarges the dimension in a way difficult to put into words, but which is far more than a function of historical accuracy. Let us consider next, therefore, a setting which is expressive, rather than naturalistic, and where the element of the self-evidently theatrical is more prominent. The text is *Krapp's Last Tape* by Samuel Beckett, first performed at the Royal Court in 1958.

A late evening in the future.

KRAPP's den.

Front centre a small table, the two drawers of which open towards the audience.

Sitting at the table, facing front, i.e. across from the drawers, a wearish old man: KRAPP.

Rusty black narrow trousers too short for him. Rusty black sleeveless waistcoat, four capacious pockets. Heavy silver watch and chain. Grimy white shirt open at neck, no collar. Surprising pair of dirty white boots, size ten at least, very narrow and pointed.

White face. Purple nose. Disordered grey hair. Unshaven.

Very near-sighted (but unspectacled). Hard of hearing.

Cracked voice. Distinctive intonation.

Laborious walk.

On the table a tape-recorder with microphone and a number of cardboard boxes containing reels of recorded tapes.

Table and immediately adjacent area in strong white light. Rest of stage in darkness.

(First S.D.)

The character at his table is in a situation quite different from that of Mary with her jumper off, reading the paper and making-up. Whereas she is in a room on a certain date (1922) surrounded by a multitude of things which tell the date, the place, her social status, the kind of life the family lead, Krapp is an isolated figure in strong white light in a dark space. That light is stage light. Beckett does not instruct the director whether he should show the actual electric lamps or not, any more than O'Casey tells us what sort of light comes through the window of the tenement. In the latter case it will be an illusion of morning light in northern Europe, in the case of Krapp it can have no other source than that of the theatre's own lamps. It is not the sun, nor a reading light. Nor is this a room with doors and windows.

We are removed at once, therefore, from time and place. To where we have been removed is problematical. Beckett writes things which we cannot see. 'A late evening in the future' is an authorial comment which suggests rather the novelist than the playwright. In fact the subsequent text of the play gives no particular indication of the date of the action except as is inciental (the presence of a tape recorder is modern, not medieval). Perhaps Beckett is suggesting something more general – this is our future. The action concerns an old man at the very end of his life, looking back upon it. 'Late evening' means 'old age'. It does not indicate time of day.

Likewise 'Krapp's den' is authorial comment, and not apparent upon stage, for we see not a room expressive of the folk who live within it, but only the small table, the two drawers which are open towards us – not towards Krapp as would be natural – and the tape recorder and reels. To this Krapp's life has been reduced. The tape recorder is necessary because some device has to be used by which Krapp may recall his earlier life. The small table has no function in itself except in so far as something is needed to stand the recorder on.

The very presence of any kind of set is a kind of distraction – what kind of table? what make of tape recorder? – because it makes us read it like the Boyle's household, as if real, whereas the set is striving towards the condition of a poetic metaphor which exists within theatre. Like all such metaphors it is difficult to translate, but the suggestion seems to be of loneliness, isolation, imminent darkness, although my choice of humanistic vocabulary here (I am describing the set as expressive of Krapp's condition) may not sufficiently acknowledge the theatrical nature of the piece, which is exploring how much may be dispensed with on the stage in making a dramatic utterance. (In the next sequence of the play Beckett uses mime.)

The dress of the character is expressive. Read naturalistically we see an elderly, old-fashioned man – the narrow black trousers, black waistcoat and silver watch and chain were not contemporary fashion in 1958. There are suggestions of the shabby genteel – the collarless white shirt is grimy, the trousers do not fit properly (have they been bought second hand?). The other details: unshaven, disordered hair, near-sighted but no glasses build up a natural portrait of the kind one might find in a Chekhov play. There is a strange tension set up, therefore, between the set, which is 'unreal', of the stage, and the character's dress which in these details would fit a real person. But that tension is carried over into the dress also: 'Surprising pair of dirty white boots, size ten at least, very narrow and pointed.' This is incongruous, and never explained in the subsequent action. What of the white face and purple nose? If this is naturalistic, it tells us Krapp drinks too much (he does). But it also suggests the formal make-up of a clown – a character of the stage. Krapp, we shall see, is a comic figure of sorts. The name itself is expressive.

What we see is 'surprising'– to use Beckett's own word – in a way that the Boyle household is not. In the Boyle's tenement we have the illusion that were we to step into a Dublin tenement of 1922, this is what we should see. But Beckett mixes here elements which are recognizable from everyday life with elements which are bizarre (and, in the case of the boots, inexplicable). The scene draws attention to its theatricality – the clown make-up, the ostensible stage lighting – so that its action will not be confined by probabilities of everyday life, but may use the language of the stage itself to express whatever it is that will follow. Surprise has stirred curiosity. The images are full of latent suggestion.

We are more familiar with this kind of theatre now than in 1958. Critical labels are soon attached to things. One might call this 'absurd' theatre compared with O'Casey's 'naturalism'. Such words are useful shorthand, if they do not obscure our capacity to look with a live eye at what is to be seen, and to be moved by it. 'Surprise' is what Beckett was after in mixing things illogically (I suspect those white boots are there because Beckett used to play cricket – but that is neither here nor there). That illogicality may be an image of the very absurdity of the universe itself – from which God has disappeared. But one should not compartmentalize too readily. O'Casey's alarm clock lying on its face is more 'absurd' than Krapp's silver watch and chain. The grandeur of the Georgian tenement room of 1922 is itself a comment on the absurdity of Irish pretension. On the other hand Krapp's use of the tape recorder to keep a diary of his past, to recall memory, is a device of naturalistic theatre which is extremely close to the naturalistic monologues of Mrs Madigan in *Juno* which begin 'I remember . . .'.

The language of theatre is extremely rich and varied. One must look with one's own eyes, hear with one's own ears and not merely attach critical labels.

Both the examples have been chosen from modern theatre because of the present custom of detailed authorial control. Although we have elaborate descriptions of seventeenth-century scene changes in court masque, and in Baroque theatre thereafter, we do not possess similar declarations of intention which involve actors closely with their environment. These matters are problematical upon the bare platform stage for which Shakespeare worked.

If the acting space is simply an empty area – a platform before a tiring house in a London entertainment centre, the floor of a Tudor hall before the hall screen in a nobleman's house (or the Queen's Court) – then the visual language of theatre is concentrated more upon properties and upon costume. The less there is upon stage, the more weight of emphasis is thrown upon the few things which can be shown there. In Marlowe's tragedy *Tamburlaine*, in the second play of that name, the conqueror's wife dies, and her body is laid in a coffin which he then takes with him wherever he goes. The black hearse which follows him clearly is a warning of death: a *memento mori*, and as such is an emblem: a visible sign carrying a moral message. The man who would conquer the whole world, even the universe itself, has forgotten that he is merely a man, and is mortal. The coffin reminds the audience of what Tamburlaine has forgotten, until, suddenly, death strikes. In Middleton's tragedy *Women Beware Women* two women, seated downstage, play chess, while out of sight, upstage, a wife (Bianca: the white lady) is corrupted. The moves which are described on the chess board we see parallel the action which we cannot see. There is a relation between the name Bianca and the white pieces, between white and purity. Even the object of the game – mate – and sexual corruption are related. In Marlowe's *Edward II* the play opens with the entry of Edward's homosexual lover Gaveston returned from overseas. It would be appropriate for him to be dressed in costume which not only expresses his amatory nature, but which is foreign fashion. The nobles of England, who hate him, are in mourning for Edward I, the great warrior king. The black of mourning will be contrasted with Gaveston's bright colours; the blazoned heraldry of the peers of England will contrast with Gaveston's lack of any similar signs of rank. This is not written into the stage directions. But such visual language is entirely appropriate to the kind of theatre of the age.

It is possible to speculate without end about the stage space itself upon which such visual signs were displayed. At the beginning of *Dr Faustus* the scholar is 'discovered' at a desk in his study. Would it be appropriate to see that desk – isolated in a stage space – as parallel to Krapp's table in its pool of white light in darkness? Both express 'study' – this is where Faustus and Krapp read and write. The absence of any other naturalistic detail might be argued to draw attention to the theatrical nature of the statement, or to the universal implication of the theme. This is not a particular man in a particular room at a particular time. The theatre shows an Everyman figure whose action is expressive of the whole human condition. In that way one may see a connection between medieval morality plays, Elizabethan theatre, and our own contemporary stage.

Such connections are enlivening. The comparative method of this study encourages them. But it is always a process of give and take. Comparison shows connection, but also encourages discrimination. There is this obvious distinction between Faustus at his desk and Krapp at his table: Beckett in 1958 is breaking from the traditions of naturalistic theatre. The 'surprise' which he seeks only exists if one expected something different. But for Marlowe and Shakespeare and all other writers for bare platform stages, the empty space was simply the expected area in which plays took place. It is neutral ground into which they introduced whatever was necessary for the action that was to be portrayed. The character Marlowe portrays is not labelled Everyman. He is called Dr Faustus, and he lives at Wittenberg, in Germany. Krapp is a generic name of sorts. The Doctor's is specific; John Faustus. We have his biography.

There is no such thing as a typical piece of theatrical writing from the age of Shakespeare which might illustrate the essential nature of the stage space. Jonson is as different from Shakespeare as Beckett from O'Casey. What will be offered for discussion is a simple piece of stage action involving the use of a property with an expressive function among characters whose appearance and costume express meaning visually. The space in which they perform is otherwise empty. The example chosen is from Marlowe's *The Jew of Malta* for which the earliest recorded performance is at the Rose theatre in 1592. The central character, the Jew, Barabas, is an energetic trickster who sets himself to be revenged on the Knights of Malta who have confiscated his wealth to buy off the Turks. The audience are kept well informed by direct address of his plots (which include mass murder of nuns by poisoned porridge). At the end Barabas does a deal with Malta's governor Ferneze to drop the Turkish leader Calymath through a trapdoor into 'a deep pit past recovery' and blow up the Turkish army; the fee, a hundred thousand pounds. The play ends thus:

A charge [sounded]; the cable cut, a cauldron discovered [into which
Barabas falls].

Calymath	How now, what means this?
Barabas	Help, help me, Christians, help!
Ferneze	See, Calymath, this was devised for thee.
Calymath	Treason, treason, bashaws, fly!
Ferneze	No, Selim, do not fly;
	See his end first, and then fly if thou canst.
Barabas	O help me, Selim, help me, Christians!
	Governor, why stand you all so pitiless?
Ferneze	Should I in pity of thy plaints or thee,
	Accursed Barabas, base Jew, relent?
	No, thus I'll see thy treachery repaid,
	But wish thou hadst behaved thee otherwise.
Barabas	You will not help me then?
Ferneze	No, villain, no.
Barabas	And, villains, know you cannot help me now.
	Then, Barabas, breathe forth thy latest fate,
	And in the fury of thy torments strive
	To end thy life with resolution.
	Know, governor, 'twas I that slew thy son;
	I framed the challenge that did make them meet.
	Know, Calymath, I aimed thy overthrow,
	And had I but escaped this stratagem
	I would have brought confusion on you all,
	Damned Christian dogs, and Turkish infidels!
	But now begins the extremity of heat
	To pinch me with intolerable pangs:
	Die, life: fly, soul; tongue, curse thy fill and die!

Calymath	Tell me, you Christians, what doth this portend?
Ferneze	This train he laid to have entrapped thy life.
	Now, Selim, note the unhallowed deeds of Jews:
	Thus he determined to have handled thee,
	But I have rather chose to save thy life.
Calymath	Was this the banquet he prepared for us?
	Let's hence, lest further mischief be pretended. . .
Ferneze	Why, heard'st thou not the trumpet sound a charge?
Calymath	Yes; what of that?
Ferneze	Why, then the house was fired,
	Blown up, and all thy soldiers massacred.
Calymath	O monstrous treason!
Ferneze	A Jew's courtesy;
	For he that did by treason work our fall
	By treason hath delivered thee to us. . .
	Content thee, Calymath, here thou must stay,
	And live in Malta prisoner; for come all the world
	To rescue thee, so will we guard us now,
	As sooner shall they drink the ocean dry,
	Than conquer Malta, or endanger us.
	So, march away, and let due praise be given
	Neither to fate nor fortune, but to heaven.

[Exeunt]

FINIS

The immediate concern of this chapter is the visual language of the stage. What effect is communicated by the appearance of the single, major property we see: the cauldron? Equally important: what do Barabas, Ferneze and Calymath look like? At the same time it would be appropriate to add to these questions matter from earlier discussion: what is the nature of the *action* we *see* here? The issues this sequence raise are analogous to the problematical scene of Christy's burning in *The Playboy*.

One piece of information must be added which the scene does not contain. It concerns Barabas's nose. He is called earlier 'bottle-nosed': he has the extremely large nose associated with the 'stage Jew'. Add to this the implication of the name Barabas (the robber who was released when Christ was crucified) then we may conclude that the character looks like an evil caricature of Jewishness. He is typical of the race (as seen anti-Semitically), just as Krapp's white face and purple nose tell us that Krapp is related to clowns. Probably, therefore, Ferneze and Calymath are also dressed equally typically, one as a Christian knight (with a red cross upon his breast), the other as a Turk. What we see, thus, are visual representatives of the three principal religions of Europe: the Jewish, Christian and Mohammedan.

The scene is an icon: it conveys a religious message. But what sort of message? Our main concern is the cauldron. Is this stage property naturalistically conceived? Or is it like a cauldron in a pantomime? Or is it hell mouth? Learned criticism of Marlowe has been much attracted by the idea. Hell mouths were standard stage properties of the time. One turns up in a relevant stage list. At the end of *Dr Faustus* the hero is carried off to hell. Barabas has spoken of 'a deep pit past recovery'. We know that Elizabethan theatre evolved from medieval moralities. We have already considered Faustus as an Everyman figure. Would it not be appropriate if that cauldron were a representation of hell – and the evil Barabas dies in it?

In this respect the cauldron is analogous to the burning of Christy: 'God help him so'. Yet, whereas Synge has surrounded the burning of Christy with explicit Christian references, Marlowe's text does not. Neither the stage direction 'a cauldron discovered' nor anything specifically said at this moment enable us confidently to say: this set represents hell mouth. The evidence is not there. What Calymath says when he sees the cauldron is 'How now, what means this?'. The suggestion may be that we are asked – how do we interpret the set? But the answer is not supplied. Marlowe tantalizes in the same way as Beckett.

A crucial question concerns the relation between the set and the way Barabas falls into the pot. It was asked of *The Playboy* is this tragedy, a farce, or tragedy for some and farce/comedy for others? So too here: are we watching a moralistic act of retribution in which an evil Jew brings about his own downfall and Christianity triumphs – or what? The authorial intention is not recorded (compare, in *Krapp*, the detailed description which follows the stage setting of how Krapp eats a banana). I suggest, and it can be no more than suggestion, that it is farce. That it is difficult for a bottle-nosed stage Jew to fall from a great height into a boiling cauldron to the accompaniment of a trumpet sound and a huge explosion in any other way than to a big shout of laughter from the audience.

If that is so, then it has a substantial effect upon the moral statements made by the Christian knight to the infidel Turk. Those moral statements will not be discussed here – are they 'straight' or are they perverted (the Christian is just as much a crook as the Jew)? Ideology is a subject we are not ready for. What a play means depends upon the nature of the theatrical action (farce or morality?) – how we read what is said here depends upon how we see the cauldron and how Barabas falls into it.

It also depends on how Barabas gets out of the pot. On a bare platform stage the cauldron would be left revealed as the cast 'march away'. What happens then? Barabas remains concealed until the audience go home? Then the actor will miss his applause. Is the pot carried out, then, or a curtain drawn before it and the actor gets out behind the curtain? Or, in full view, the actor gets out of the pot to take his applause – reminding us that this is a play we have seen, an entertainment. (So, at the end of one production of *The Playboy* the actor playing Old Mahon removed his damaged scalp – it was a comic stage property.) Or does *Barabas*, the character, get out of the cauldron and make his exit – having tricked the Christians once again? – an ingenious theatrical resolution.

The text does not tell us. But there the cauldron stands. Something must be done with it upon the empty space. What solution do you find best?

3 Genre

If you want to know about plays, then you must read and see many plays. That is what playwrights do. Nothing is made of nothing. All writers inherit from their predecessors a series of conventions of form, ways of using language, which are the building blocks from which they work. Sometimes those conventions are so much the common property of the times that they seem instinctively right, as if they were 'natural'. At other times they appear stale, artificial, empty and conventions and speech are revitalized by 'original genius'. Our analogy with the wheelwright holds good. Ask a man to make a wheel and the mind may invoke all the kinds of wheel which are known. But what kind of wheel do we want? For a cart? A motor car? 'Original genius' conceived the caterpillar track. But it remains a wheel, varied.

Contemporary cinema is the most obvious repository of conventional forms (genre) today: the western, the Hollywood musical, the spy thriller, vampire film, space-war epic. The titles frequently point to the genre: *Stage Coach, The Sound of Music, The Kremlin Letter, Star Wars*. Any cinema-goer knows what to expect. The forms have particular conventions appropriate to the genre. It is pointless to ask why the sheriff challenges the gunman to 'draw'. In the western 'a man's got to do what a man's got to do'. The use of such conventions is of great value to the artist. They may serve as a way of short-cutting the plot: 'One enchanted evening, you will see a stranger. . .' (boy meets girl; instant romantic love); or the existence of the expectation which the convention arouses can be used to surprise that expectation. A recent low-budget movie, *Westworld*, combined the genres of the western and sci-fi. A holiday camp of androids had been created in which the humanized robots were programmed to perform the stock situations of the western.

The holiday makers then were allowed to act out their fantasies – for instance by out-drawing the chief gunman (who was programmed to lose). But then the androids rebelled. . . .

Theatre has always used devices of this kind. Nor should 'English literature' be separated from popular culture. Plays were popular before they became 'literature' in the academic sense. Two of the most common generic types of theatre have already been introduced without explanation: tragedy and comedy. Eric Bentley in *The Life of Drama* argues that more fundamental than these are the popular forms farce and melodrama. The labels multiply and subdivide endlessly. Remember Polonius:

The best actors in the world, either for tragedy, comedy, history, pastoral, pastoral–comical, historical–pastoral, tragical–historical, tragical–comical–historical–pastoral. . . .

(*Hamlet* II. ii. 424–7)

If one thinks of contemporary cinema, and a mixed-genre film like *Westworld* one sees at once Polonius's problem. Later criticism has spawned many other labels: Revenge Tragedy, Restoration Comedy, Problem Play, Absurdist Theatre.

It is not our function to write a dictionary of forms, nor an anatomy of theatre. Aristotle began it. What was for him descriptive (this is what playwrights do) for later critics became prescriptive (this is what should be done): the famous 'Rules' of neoclassical criticism which everyone but scholars has now forgotten. In our own times critics like Northrop Frye have attempted to make an anatomy of Shakespeare's comedies. Since Shakespeare frequently repeated himself, he made (and broke) his own conventions.

One such convention in comedy has already emerged in this discussion. Comedies of love usually end with marriage (or the confirmation of marriage): so Shakespeare, *A Midsummer Night's Dream*; Congreve, *Love for Love*; Wilde, *The Importance of Being Earnest*. That is why it is ridiculous to ask why Olivia marries Sebastian at the end of *Twelfth Night*. What would be significant is if she did not. Which is what happens in *The Playboy of the Western World*. Until Pegeen burns Christy's leg their relation has followed the convention of love comedy: boy and girl will marry. After that moment, their marriage is impossible. The convention is destroyed.

Shakespeare makes a similar twist at the end of *Love's Labour's Lost*, and draws attention to it: 'Our wooing doth *not* end like an old play; Jack hath not Jill'. Conversely Congreve in *The Way of the World*, an intrigue comedy full of dark overtones and stress, firmly points to the coming happy resolution in the penultimate scene when the comic Witwoud declares, 'Hey day! What are you all got together, like players at the end of the last act?'.

It is doubtful, however, if there is much value in seeking to define genre too precisely. Either one ends in a banal generality like 'Comedies end fortunately, tragedies unfortunately' or in such complex description that exceptions begin to seem the norm. Even Northrop Frye, with Shakespeare's comedies, cannot make everything fit. The analogy from anatomy holds good. Men and women have, in large measure, similar skeletons which distinguish the human species from earthworms. The bones of Adolph Hitler and Marilyn Monroe are not greatly dissimilar. Yet, for anyone but the anatomist, it is the difference between the people which is most striking.

There are no easy answers. Conventions exist. Not to recognize them is to misread. To see only the conventions is to be blind to the individual hand of the craftsman. The only way to learn about these things is the way the writers themselves adopted: to read. Congreve's *The Way of the World* changes before your eyes if you know Etherege's *The Man of Mode*. There is a certain kind of hero peculiar to both plays: the rake. Read further in the theatre of the time and the figure appears in many places (so figures such as Flash Gordon, Luke Skywalker, Indiana Jones are common to our culture). In Congreve the figure of the rake changes. He is reformed. The play is a comment upon a tradition.

It is easier to give specific example of a particular generic convention than to discourse on the nature of tragedy or comedy in general. The first illustration is drawn from a subgenre of tragedy: the revenge play – of which *Hamlet* is the best-known example. In this kind of play an evil deed demands evil in reply: murder is to be revenged by murder. Chapman, Kyd, Marston, Tourneur are contemporaries of Shakespeare who wrote variations of this form. One device used within this genre is that of the ghost. Shakespeare probably had seen, or read, the following. It is the Prologue to Thomas Kyd's *The Spanish Tragedy*. Compare the beginning of *Hamlet*.

Enter the Ghost of Andrea, *and with him* Revenge.

Ghost   When this eternal substance of my soul
         Did live imprison'd in my wanton flesh,
         Each in their function serving other's need,
         I was a courtier in the Spanish court:
         My name was Don Andrea; my descent,
         Though not ignoble, yet inferior far
         To gracious fortunes of my tender youth.
         For there in prime and pride of all my years,
         By duteous service and deserving love,
         In secret I possess'd a worthy dame,
         Which hight sweet Bellimperia by name.
         But, in the harvest of my summer joys,
         Death's winter nipp'd the blossoms of my bliss,
         Forcing divorce betwixt my love and me.
         For on the late conflict with Portugal
         Thy valour drew me into danger's mouth,
         Till life to death made passage through my wounds,
         When I was slain, my soul descended straight
         To pass the flowing stream of Acheron;
         But churlish Charon, only boatman there,
         Said that, my rites of burial not perform'd
         I might not sit amongst his passengers
         Ere Sol had slept three nights in Thetis' lap,
         And slak'd his smoking chariot in her flood,
         By Don Horatio, our knight marshal's son,
         My funerals and obsequies were done. . .
         [He describes the underworld]
         Forthwith, Revenge, She [Prosperina, queen of the
                             underworld] rounded thee in th'ear,
         And bade thee lead me through the gates of horn,
         Where dreams have passage in the silent night.
         No sooner had she spoke, but we were here –
         I wot not how – in twinkling of an eye.

Revenge Then know, Andrea, that thou art arriv'd
         Where thou shalt see the author of thy death,
         Don Balthazar, the prince of Portugal,
         Depriv'd of life by Bellimperia.
         Here sit we down to see the mystery,
         And serve for Chorus in this tragedy.

Francisco *at his post. Enter to him* Bernardo.

Bernardo	Who's there?
Francisco	Nay, answer me: stand, and unfold youself.
Bernardo	Long live the king!
Francisco	Bernardo?
Bernardo	He.
Francisco	You come most carefully upon your hour.
Bernardo	'Tis now struck twelve; get thee to bed, Francisco.
Francisco	For this relief, much thanks; 'tis bitter cold,
	And I am sick at heart.
Bernardo	Have you had quiet guard?
Francisco	Not a mouse stirring.
Bernardo	Well, good-night.
	If you do meet Horatio and Marcellus,
	The rivals of my watch, bid them make haste.
Francisco	I think I hear them. Stand, ho! Who's there?

Enter Horatio *and* Marcellus.

Horatio	Friends to this ground.
Marcellus	And liegemen to the Dane.
Francisco	Give you good-night.
Marcellus	O! farewell honest soldier:
	Who hath reliev'd you?
Francisco	Bernardo has my place.
	Give you good night. *[Exit]*
Marcellus	Holla! Bernardo!
Bernardo	Say,
	What! is Horatio there?
Horatio	A piece of him.
Bernardo	Welcome, Horatio; welcome, good Marcellus.
Marcellus	What! has this thing appear'd again tonight?
Bernardo	I have seen nothing.
Marcellus	Horatio says 'tis but our fantasy,
	And will not let belief take hold of him
	Touching this dreaded sight twice seen of us:
	Therefore I have entreated him along
	With us to watch the minutes of this night;
	That if again this apparition come,
	He may approve our eyes and speak to it.

Horatio	Tush, tush! 'twill not appear.
Bernardo	Sit down awhile,
	And let us once again assail your ears,
	That are so fortified against our story,
	What we two nights have seen.
Horatio	Well, sit we down,
	And let us hear Bernardo speak of this.
Bernardo	Last night of all,
	When yond same star that's westward from the pole
	Had made his course to illume that part of heaven
	Where now it burns, Marcellus and myself,
	The bell then beating one, –
Marcellus	Peace! break thee off; look, where it comes again!

Enter Ghost.

The manner in which Kyd introduces his play is so formal that it reads almost as if it were a programme note telling us about the historical background. Andrea is not engaged in an action but a recitation: 'I was a courtier in the Spanish court:/My name was Don Andrea'. Such direct address is a common device of the 1590s – Shakespeare uses it, for instance, to introduce *Richard III*. But Richard's speech to the audience gives reasons why a man who cannot play a 'lover' is determined to play a 'villain'. There seems no reason why Andrea should be telling us anything, for nothing is going to be performed by this character – he is going to sit down and watch the play with us. The function of the speech remains that of a programme note. It introduces us to various characters who will have a part in the action: Bellimperia and Don Horatio. It is the murder of Don Horatio by Balthazar which leads to Heronimo (Horatio's father) and Bellimperia revenging themselves upon Balthazar and thus, indirectly, revenging Andrea. Although we are enticed to wonder what is about to happen, the introduction of the characters is so clumsy that Andrea even neglects to name Heronimo, who is the 'knight marshal' of the prologue. Indeed most of the prologue is taken up with a description of the underworld which may show the playwright's classical learning, but has nothing to do with the action at all.

The costumes, perhaps, are more expressive than the language. Andrea is dressed as 'Ghost' and by him stands a sinister, and mainly silent, figure whom the eye must read as 'Revenge'. What we see tells us that this is tragedy in general, and revenge tragedy in particular. The action of sitting down (compare the watch in *Hamlet*) is more significant than much of the bombast about the underworld. If members of the audience were upon the edge of the platform where the action occurs, then the Ghost and Revenge sit down among them as spectators. This would seem to tell us both that this is 'only' a play we are watching, and yet involves us with the action of the play. Shakespeare uses exactly such a device in the player scene in *Hamlet* when the old-style tragedy – which is so much like this play by Kyd – is performed among the spectators at Elsinore who, like us, the audience, are watchers of the play, yet moved to action by it.

The Ghost of Andrea is the 'parent' of Hamlet's father's ghost. The appearance of the supernatural being is the sign that this is a revenge tragedy which is to be played. When the Ghost in *Hamlet* eventually speaks, his language is not dissimilar from the formality of Kyd:

> I am thy father's spirit;
Doom'd for a certain term to walk the night,
And for the day confin'd to fast in fires. . .

but everything else is changed, for the Ghost is involved in the action, and in agonized dialogue with his son. But at the beginning the skill of the craftsman resides in the way the appearance of the spirit is delayed, and even the information that we are awaiting a ghost is held back.

Kyd, relying upon formal convention, makes little use of the stage space: the Ghost advances, speaks, sits down. Shakespeare, at the change of the watch, using two groups of people, immediately involves the players in an action which converts the empty space into a 'ground' over which guard and relief have to move (to change the watch). In so doing we learn not only the place of the action – these are the battlements of some fortified place (the men are dressed as soldiers) – but also the extreme tension of the watchmen is communicated.

It would be redundant to analyse the swift and agitated movement of the dialogue (verbal action and reaction) from the very beginning: 'Who's there?' 'Nay, answer *me*'. It is easy to see also, on the elementary but fundamental level, the way in which names are introduced and characters involved in the situation (compare the crudity of Kyd's programme notes): 'unfold yourself.' 'Long live the king!' 'Bernardo?' 'He.' (That exclamation 'Long live the king!' will soon acquire ironic significance.) I would hope also, by now, that the student might ask, is Horatio dressed as a soldier? (probably not) and the way, therefore, his difference in costume indicates his different function. The military costume of the watch, too, like the garb of Revenge in Kyd, is communicating information: images of war and violence which will run throughout the play, and be repeated at the very end when Fortinbras enters with his soldiers to take over the Danish state. How much more, therefore, Shakespeare extracts from what is seen and said.

The (conventional) Ghost is not mentioned until line 21, and then only indirectly 'What! has this *thing* appear'd tonight?' and immediately the verbal act meets with reaction. Not only has Bernardo seen nothing, but Horatio (courtier, not soldier, and their social and intellectual superior) is revealed as an unbeliever. At least, Marcello says Horatio does not believe. What Horatio says is 'Tush, tush! 'twill not appear.' That is susceptible of more than one interpretation. Perhaps the alarm has spread to him, and he hopes the 'thing' will not come tonight. Then Bernardo begins to give us a piece of Kyd. He launches into what is clearly going to be a long formal set speech to tell the audience in the proper high, 'poetic' style, all about the appearance of Revenge Tragedy ghosts. He has not completed five lines (Kyd allowed himself more than 80), and when we least expect it, and at a part of the stage where we are not looking, the 'thing' appears. Envisage the reaction.

But the Ghost in Hamlet is pure convention. It belongs to Revenge Tragedy, and is in *Hamlet* because of Kyd and whatever other progenitors of the form Shakespeare knew. Its presence tells us what kind of play we are watching, and what to expect. The craft lies in the astonishing things that the playwright then does with the material that tradition puts into his hands. First there is expectation. Then surprise. It has not been done like that before. Kyd is a poor writer (in this extract), and Shakespeare a very good one. But without Kyd there would not be this kind of first scene in *Hamlet*. You need the form before you can work with it.

(A brief book compels brevity in discussion. If this is read by a group it would be useful to get up, create an empty space, and perform these two scenes. Consider the use of the space; the appearance of the actors; the physical and verbal action and reaction within the space (the relation of movement and speech); the manner in which the climax is built – expectation and suspense.)

This first example of generic convention has been chosen from plays closely related in time. It is possible to see relation also between works separated by centuries. Comedy, for instance, has often utilized a limited number of repeated (stock) situations and characters. If the comic dramatists of the Greek world were to return to life they would see much that was familiar in the work of Joe Orton. But a history of comic theatre would not serve the practical purposes of this discussion. Let it suffice to note that much of the comic drama of Europe derives from Graeco-Roman tradition and from the *commedia dell'arte*. Thus, the Roman dramatist Plautus utilized a character called the *miles gloriosus* (the braggart soldier – who is really a coward). There is the origin of Falstaff and of Christy Mahon in *The Playboy*. It would be a more practical task to take a highly traditional comedy such as *The Importance of Being Earnest* (1895) and place it against an earlier work of love intrigue, say *A Midsummer Night's Dream* (?1595). Consider how many formal elements they have in common. The use of marriage as a resolution has been cited already. In both there is a parental block to a desired marriage; a conflict between the generations; a movement from the town to the country; a comedy of mistaken identities. Each of these themes is traditional. One might explore, for instance, the function of Theseus in Shakespeare, and that of Lady Bracknell in Wilde. How is the common material altered, and for what purposes?

The example for discussion is simpler. Both plays use the device known popularly as the eternal triangle. In this case two young women believe they are in love with the same man, and quarrel. Shakespeare's action occurs in the usual 'empty space' of his age (perhaps a nobleman's hall, for the work may celebrate a specific marriage). Wilde wrote for the St James's Theatre, and for a naturalistic set within a proscenium arch.

Hermia	O me! you juggler! you canker-blossom!
	You thief of love! what! have you come by night
	And stol'n my love's heart from him?

Helena	Fine, i'faith!
	Have you no modesty, no maiden shame,
	No touch of bashfulness? What! will you tear
	Impatient answers from my gentle tongue?
	Fie, fie! You counterfeit, you puppet you!
Hermia	Puppet! why, so: ay, that way goes the game.
	Now I perceive that she hath made compare
	Between our statures: she hath urg'd her height;
	And with her personage, her tall personage,
	Her height, forsooth, she hath prevail'd with him.
	Are are you grown so high in his esteem,
	Because I am so dwarfish and so low?
	How low am I, thou painted maypole? speak;
	How low am I? I am not yet so low
	But that my nails can reach unto thine eyes.
Helena	I pray you, though you mock me, gentlemen,
	Let her not hurt me: I was never curst;
	I have no gift at all in shrewishness;
	I am a right maid for my cowardice:
	Let her not strike me. You perhaps may think,
	Because she is something lower than myself,
	That I can match her.
Hermia	Lower! hark, again!

(III.ii.282–305)

Cecily	(*rather shy and confidingly*) Dearest Gwendolen, there is no reason why I should make a secret of it to you. Our little county newspaper is sure to chronicle the fact next week. Mr Ernest Worthing and I are engaged to be married.
Gwendolen	(*quite politely, rising and moving to C*) My darling Cecily, I think there must be some slight error. Mr Ernest Worthing is engaged to me. The announcement will appear in the *Morning Post* on Saturday at the latest.
Cecily	(*very politely, rising and moving to RC*) I am afraid you must be under some misconception. Ernest proposed to me exactly ten minutes ago. (*She shows her diary*)
Gwendolen	(*examining the diary carefully through her lorgnette*) It is certainly very curious, for he asked *me* to be his wife

yesterday afternoon at five-thirty. If you would care to verify the incident, pray do so. I never travel without my diary. (*She produces a diary of her own*) One should always have something sensational to read in the train. I am so sorry, dear Cecily, if it is any disappointment to you, but I am afraid *I* have the prior claim.

Cecily   It would distress me more than I can tell you, dear Gwendolen, if it caused you any mental or physical anguish, but I feel bound to point out that since Ernest proposed to *you* he clearly has changed his mind.

Gwendolen   (*meditatively*) If the poor fellow has been entrapped into any foolish promise I shall consider it my duty to rescue him *at once*, and with a *firm hand*.

Cecily   (*thoughtfully and sadly, moving slowly R*) Whatever unfortunate entanglement my dear boy may have got into, *I* will never reproach him with it *after* we are married.

Gwendolen   Do you allude to *me*, Miss Cardew, as an entanglement? You are presumptuous. On an occasion of this kind it becomes more than a moral duty to speak one's mind. It becomes a pleasure.

Cecily   (*moving back to RC*) Do you suggest, Miss Fairfax, that I entrapped Ernest into an engagement? How dare you? This is no time for wearing the shallow mask of manners. When I see a *spade* I call it a *spade*.

Gwendolen   (*satirically, up LC*) I am glad to say that I have never seen a spade. It is obvious that our social spheres have been *widely* different.

(*Merriman enters C*)

(Act II)

The similarities within difference are striking. First the action. To move a potentially serious action (a jealous quarrel) into comedy both writers have pushed the actors into extremes. Shakespeare uses the more obvious device. We are on the threshold of a girl fight and close, therefore, to the kind of fundamental theatre represented by *Trafford Tanzi*: the wrestling match. Anyone who will move the action of this scene will appreciate at once how much it gives the lie to the view that formal blank verse imposes a corresponding formal stiffness upon the players. What in fact happens upon a bare stage is that the empty space concentrates the actors' speech and movement upon each other (there are no distracting things to fiddle with, like teapots). One notices that it is the tall blonde girl who is afraid, while the smaller, dark girl is the aggressor. The disparity heightens the comedy. But we know little else about the characters than that one is tall and the other short, one fair, one dark. They are depersonalized. Admitted that in a moment Helen adds 'She was a vixen when she went to school'. A naturalistic touch like that is typical of Shakespeare, but it is only a touch. The emphasis is not on 'character' but on situation: the conflict between the two girls. Those who know the play will appreciate why. One moment a young man loves a tall fair girl, the next a short dark one. That is the nature of young folks' hearts. But the depersonalization aids the comedy. If these girls were heart and soul involved in their situation, driven even to violence by it, this would not be funny.

The action in Wilde is at the opposite extreme. On the naturalistic stage he has given his players 'distracting things to fiddle with, like tea-pots'. Cecily, the country girl, is entertaining Gwendolen, the town miss, to afternoon tea in the garden. But, of course, they do not 'fiddle'. The presence of the tea table between them enables Wilde to use it to impose the decorum of respectability upon two girls of the upper classes (one dressed as the country miss, the other in the fashion of the town). They would like a fight, but instead the situation forces them into scrupulous extremes of politeness. The comedy is in the extreme (as with Shakespeare). It is much too polite. The action of getting up from the table, before tea is finished, is indicative of the extremity of the tension. By the end of the sequence, when both girls are on their feet, and hot under the bodice, we ought to feel on the very verge of a breakdown of the social forms, and Wilde at this moment brings in the servant to clear the table (and restrain the girls).

As with Shakespeare the characters are depersonalized. It is town girl and country girl. Those who know the play will point out, correctly, that Gwendolen is a young version of Lady Bracknell. When she is old and ugly instead of young and pretty her husband will find her just as much a gorgon. But that is a thematic device of the play: many of the characters are mirror images one of another. The most obvious thing about Cecily and Gwendolen here is that they parallel one another.

Gwendolen rises, and moves to one part of the stage. Cecily rises, and moves to another. Cecily produces a diary. Gwendolen produces a diary. (If read in a group this action should be moved, this time not in an empty space as *Hamlet*, but about a table and two chairs.) What Wilde is giving us is the formality of a dance in which partners reproduce each other's moves. Another moment someone will spoil it by stamping on a toe. The expectation is built up – and denied. (So, in Shakespeare, the fight does not take place.) This use of form blocks the heart- and soul-searching which would disintegrate the comedy.

The use of dialogue in both instances both creates the movement and mirrors it. The best way to test this is to play it, for this short commentary would plod for too long in spelling out everything. The Shakespeare begins by aiming at a certain formal verse balance. Both girls use a kind of rhetoric which sets up Wildean mirror images: 'O me! you juggler! you canker blossom!/You thief of love!'... 'Have you no modesty, no maiden shame,/No touch of bashfulness?' But just as the physical action (let's have a fight) breaks decorum, so too the attempt to trade formal speeches breaks down. 'Fie, fie! You counterfeit, you puppet you' just about manages to hang on to the iambic pentameter. 'Puppet! why, so: ay, that way goes the game' all but disintegrates the verse in fury. Hermia attempts to get back to normality, as she tries to recover her temper in the middle of the speech: 'Are you grown so high in his esteem,/Because I am so dwarfish and so low?' She can play with words but then her rage gets the better of her 'How low am I, thou painted maypole? speak;/How low am I. . .?' and then, in the last line of the extract, the line is split, with 'Lower!' from Hermia stopping Helena after five syllables.

Propriety of conventional speech in Wilde provides the kind of norm which the iambic pentameter gives Shakespeare. Gradually the two characters force their way out of it. 'My *darling* Cecily, I think there must be some slight error'... 'some misconception'... 'I am so sorry, *dear* Cecily, if it is any disappointment'... 'It would distress me more than I can tell you, *dear* Gwendolen'... 'foolish promise'... 'unfortunate entanglement'... 'You are presumptuous'... 'How dare you?' (that breaks decorum without doubt) – thence to the threat to speak directly 'When I see a *spade* I call it a *spade*' and then Gwendolen's famous verbal climax (which wins the round).

The timing of this is all important. Raise the temperature too soon and it goes over the top. The art is sustaining the crescendo for the right length and then resolving it. In Wilde Merriman provides the break. In Shakespeare Helena runs away, and all four actors (the two young men are also on stage) abruptly depart in diverse directions (in six lines).

Wilde is neither imitating Shakespeare, nor alluding to him. Both writers are using some of the stock devices of the comic genre to build with in their particular way. The more theatre one sees the more the sense of a web of inter-relation develops, so that to touch one strand sets up resonances that run throughout the whole. Works of literature enrich one another in this way, and set up patterns of association which are not formally written into the text (not what we call an *allusion*, which is a direct reference by one literary work to another as in *Rosencrantz and Guildenstern*), but which are like the ripples in a pond, stretching ever wider until we do not know where they die, or like the resonances of a bell ringing and echoing across the countryside. There is a famous moment in the nineteenth-century tragic dramatist Ibsen when Mrs Alving hears her son laughing off stage and uncorking wine with the young dependant of the household, the girl Regine. Mrs Alving's life has been built on a lie. She has covered up for her dead husband who was a promiscuous drunkard. Her shocked reaction reveals what was until then concealed: that Regine is her son's illegitimate half sister. Mrs Alving says, 'Ghosts! Those two in the conservatory. . . come back to haunt us.' That word 'Ghosts' (the title of the play) will, for the reader of this chapter, set up associations which lead to *Hamlet* – this is how the past revenges itself now. For those who have read Greek tragedy also, the curse upon families which carries on between generations will be recalled. Ibsen's play takes its place in an ancient generic tradition.

The examples have been chosen from simple genres: tragedy, comedy and kept to particular illustration. There is no limit to which structural affiliation cannot be pushed. Some have sought for a grammar of theatre, or of all art, which underlies all particular expression. It is like the quest of Mr Casaubon in *Middlemarch* for a key to all the mythologies, and is often linked to the origins of theatre in myth or ritual, or in the fundamental nature of the human psyche. Two such explorers have already been named: Eric Bentley and Northrop

Frye. The cycle of winter and summer, or the relation of parent and child, or the distinction between masculine and feminine provide typical organizing ideas. There are depths below depths. Consider the implications of a title like *A Midsummer Night's Dream* – midsummer and fertility myth and ritual; dream and the human psyche.

But to embark upon such discussion and examine the validity of such conceptions requires immense reading. Plot summaries, separated from the immediacy of experience, can be facilely organized into patterns; archetypal myth (typical, or perfect specimen of myth) is so vague that almost anything can be fitted in. (Of course romantic comedies are 'fertility myths'. They are about sex.) The difficulty and generality of such discussion is not for an introduction. The only way to learn about plays, I repeat, is to read and see plays. As knowledge replaces ignorance a process of adjustment occurs by comparison. One gets to recognize the craft. One sees how things change, yet relate, in history.

4 Character

'She was a vixen when she went to school' said Helen of Hermia. There was a time when a remark like that was treasured as evidence for *The Girlhood of Shakespeare's Heroines*. Doubtless Hermia kept her locker untidy too, and had grubby finger-nails. Such a silly approach to Shakespeare's characters was thrown out of the window 50 years ago. To ask a question like 'How many children had Lady Macbeth?' is to invite ridicule from the sophisticated.

Yet there is a simple fact about all theatre. It is an embodied action; the actor impersonates somebody. One of the first questions an actor will ask is 'how do I create this role?' The actor has got to move, to speak, even to give an impression of thought (the sub-text). Unless there is somebody there to impersonate, nothing is going to happen. Plays are not oratorios in which the singers stand still. They are not like announcements of plane departures in which tone of voice, emotion, personal motive are irrelevant. No one would wish to deny the importance, for instance, of the patterns of imagery in Shakespeare's verse or his ideas, themes, sources. But first there is character in action. Consider a line like 'How now! a rat? Dead, for a ducat, dead' spoken by Hamlet killing Polonius behind the arras. The line is an instruction to character in action. It is *not* given to Hamlet merely to add another animal image to the many in the play. Move it and see how the words control the component aspects of the deed. The actor will rightly ask, *how* does Hamlet move? He will also enquire *why* does he move? This is dramatic poetry. To deny the how and the why of the actor is as silly as to speculate about the contents of Hermia's school locker.

Certain constraints operate upon the way roles are created by playwrights. There is no need to waste time on the obvious. We know characters in plays are not real people. We know actors create the roles. In certain kinds of play, however, we like to watch *as if* the characters were real. That phrase *as if* provided a key in the great naturalistic director Stanislavski's approach to theatre. Hamlet acts *as if* he were really killing a man he calls a rat. The actor does not tip us a wink to let us know it is all make believe. We do make believe, and thus we believe in Hamlet's character.

Our concern is with craft: the way playwrights create roles. Certain constraints govern the nature of that *as if*. One is genre. Papageno in comedy does not set about killing himself like Othello in tragedy. Action, words, and therefore character are different. Style, thus, is also a determinant. Romeo, about to woo Juliet, cries 'But, soft! what light through yonder window breaks?/ It is the east, and Juliet is the sun!' In Chekhov's naturalistic tragi-comedy *The Cherry Orchard* Lopakhin, who is thinking about proposing to Vanya, takes out his watch, consults it, and says 'Yes'. Both speeches tell us a great deal about the state of mind of the wooer, but it would be insensitive to adopt a mode of character analysis which abstracted Romeo from the ardency of his Petrarchan verse – he speaks the language of idealized courtly love – or Lopakhin from his inarticulate prosaicness. A third determinant is function. Speeches by characters have a part to play in the structure of a play as a whole. They are not necessarily there to carry information about the person speaking, but to communicate information or ideas necessary for the structure of the play as a whole. (We all know the situation in 'coarse acting' in which the maid servant whose only function is to tell us 'Dr Smith has come, ma'am' suddenly appears as a one-legged hunchback with cross eyes, a long blonde wig and a pronounced Welsh accent!)

The functional speech needs further examination because Shakespeare frequently combines profound characterization with functionalism. To get the emphasis wrong can be misleading. In *Hamlet* Gertrude tells Laertes of his sister Ophelia's death by drowning. The tense dramatic nature of the situation and dialogue needs no emphasis. But in reply to Laertes's 'Drown'd? O, where?' Gertrude says:

There is a willow grows aslant a brook,
That shows his hoar leaves in the glassy stream;
There with fantastic garlands did she come,

Of crow-flowers, nettles, daisies, and long purples,
That liberal shepherds give a grosser name,
But our cold maids do dead men's fingers call them:
There, on the pendant boughs her coronet weeds
Clambering to hang, an envious sliver broke,
When down her weedy trophies and herself
Fell in the weeping brook. Her clothes spread wide,
And, mermaid-like, awhile they bore her up;
Which time she chanted snatches of old tunes. . .
Till that her garments, heavy with their drink,
Pull'd the poor wretch from her melodious lay
To muddy death.   (IV.vii.167–83)

If we read this as a speech like real life and as revelatory of
Gertrude's character then some very odd things follow.
Clearly, Gertrude was an observer of the scene. She knows
what flowers Ophelia carried, how she fell out of the willow,
and how she drifted down the stream singing songs. Yet
Gertrude has done nothing to pull her out of the water! How
can this be? Is Gertrude jealous of Hamlet's love for Ophelia,
and is glad, therefore, to see the rival for her affection die? How
profoundly Shakespeare has prefigured Freud! Or, perhaps,
there is a message for feminists here. In Elizabethan society
women were taught to view themselves as a helpless sexual
chattel. Thus, when Gertrude sees Ophelia drowning, she is
inhibited by her helplessness as a woman from intervening to
save her. Or is there yet another potential in the speech here?
The play concerns a man who talks about action, but does not
act. Does this speech show mother like son? Instead of doing
anything, the Queen makes beautiful poetry out of it.

This is utter rubbish. It comes from reading the passage as if
it were nineteenth-century naturalism and viewing the function of all speeches as revealing character. On the contrary, the
function of this speech is analagous to Don Andrea's prologue
in *The Spanish Tragedy*. It is there to communicate information
as if by chorus to Laertes, *and* to the audience. Accordingly it is
not fundamentally 'in character' even though the illusion of
characters in dialogue is maintained. One would do far better
to ask about the significance of the obscene flowers which
parody a pastoral elegy (compare *Lycidas*) than to wildly
speculate about Freud. The very absurdity of the specula-
tions about character should be sufficient warning that a

psychological reading here puts one on the wrong track.

Let us consider next a speech in which functionalism and character combine in Shakespeare in monologue; and then a monologue by a modern craftsman. Edmund in *King Lear* is a villain. He is plotting to dispossess his brother. He plans to get on in the world. He is also a sexually attractive young man – the plot makes clear his attractiveness to women. The other extract is from a character we have already met: Krapp. At the end of the play he is listening to the voice of his young self on a tape recorder talking of the year's events. Young Krapp is reporting the end of a love affair. In a punt one afternoon he has noticed scratches on his mistress. They came from picking gooseberries, she says. (It would be useful to voice the speeches.)

Edmund   Thou, Nature, art my goodess; to thy law
My services are bound. Wherefore should I
Stand in the plague of custom, and permit
The curiosity of nations to deprive me,
For that I am some twelve or fourteen moonshines
Lag of a brother? Why bastard? wherefore base?
When my dimensions are as well compact,
My mind as generous, and my shape as true,
As honest madam's issue? Why brand they us
With base? with baseness? bastardy? base, base?
Who in the lusty stealth of nature take
More composition and fierce quality
Than doth, within a dull, stale, tired bed,
Go to the creating a whole tribe of fops,
Got 'tween asleep and wake? Well then,
Legitimate Edgar, I must have your land:
Our father's love is to the bastard Edmund
As to the legitimate. Fine word, 'legitimate'!
Well, my legitimate, if this letter speed
And my invention thrive, Edmund the base
Shall top the legitimate: – I grow, I prosper;
Now, gods, stand up for bastards!   (I.ii.1–22)

Tape   – gooseberries, she said. I said again I thought it was hopeless and no good going on and she agreed, without opening her eyes. (*Pause.*) I asked her to look at me and

after a few moments – (*pause*) – after a few moments she
did, but the eyes just slits, because of the glare. I bent over
her to get them in the shadow and they opened. (*Pause. Low.*)
Let me in. (*Pause.*) We drifted in among the flags and stuck.
The way they went down, sighing, before the stem! (*Pause.*) I
lay down across her with my face in her breasts and my hand
on her. We lay there without moving. But under us all moved,
and moved us, gently, up and down, and from side to side.
Pause. Krapp's lips move. No sound.
Past midnight. Never knew such silence. The earth might
be uninhabited.
Pause.
Here I end this reel. Box – (*pause*) – three, spool – (*pause*)
– five. (*Pause.*) Perhaps my best years are gone. When
there was a chance of happiness. But I wouldn't want them
back. Not with the fire in me now. No, I wouldn't want
them back.

Krapp *motionless staring before him. The tape runs on in silence.*

Part of the potential of Edmund's speech can only be imagined. It comes from the embodiment of the young man by an
actor. There is the sexual attractiveness of youth, and there is
the villainy: attraction and repulsion together. The presence of
the contradiction is a major factor in making the speech dramatic. To make the villain merely villainous belongs to melodrama, or mere propaganda. The audience are implicated by the
attractiveness, and by the argument, for the speech is direct
audience address. (That cannot be proved. It could be played
introspectively, and we 'overhear' as it were. But the force of the
rhetoric from the very beginning: 'Thou, Nature, art my goodess' and the string of questions 'Why bastard? wherefore base?'
sound more like public utterance than self-examination.)

As readers we can only imagine the necessary presence of
an attractive young man. The speech itself is constructed from
three conventional elements. It contains within it a formal
expression of doctrine upon the subject of 'Nature'. This is one
of the main themes of the play which asks 'what is the nature of
man? what is the nature of Nature? is there a moral and divine
Nature?' Edmund is what is called a 'natural' child – a bastard – and therefore was begotten outside the moral law of
marriage. He follows what he calls Nature which has given him
'fierce quality'. The law of Nature is that the 'fierce' will

overcome the 'fop' (today we call it the survival of the fittest). A function of the speech is to communicate this doctrine which is part of the moral debate of the play as a whole. Read on this level the lines describe the part which the character will play thematically. They are not primarily self-revelation but rather a kind of moral label.

A second element Shakespeare uses is of the theatre, and theatrical. Edmund is 'the villain'. He is, therefore, a type. It is a convention of stage villains of the time that they are 'Machiavellian': they believe might is right and cunningly plot to deceive or destroy the virtuous. That phrase 'my invention thrive' tells the audience he is that kind of trickster. In a moment we learn he has forged a letter from his brother Edgar claiming Edgar plots against his father. Shortly he stages a false fight with Edgar. So conventional are the devices that were it not heresy to criticise *Lear* I would suggest that this side of things is stale, tired, and boringly predictable. Shakespeare merely leans on convention to hurry to more interesting things.

But both the doctrine, and the typical villainy, are humanized by the presence of the actor who speaks to us from such a 'well compact' and true shaped body. The way the questions are put suggests not 'doctrine' but plausible, personal questions. 'Why bastard? wherefore base?' We can *see* how attractive he is. 'Why brand they us/With base? with baseness? bastardy? base, base?' The repetitions are obsessive. They sound *as if* the mind were in turmoil with itself. We follow the processes of that mind. It develops a train of thought leading to the 'Well then. . .'. Edmund is thinking through a position part obsessed with his bastardy, part stimulated with a direct, personalized jealousy of that dull, stale, tired, foppish offspring, his brother 'legitimate Edgar'. Notice the emphasis that word 'legitimate' acquires. Of course it is there for doctrinal purposes (a theme of the play) but it is informed with hatred and contempt through a psychological process in which we are caught up – Edmund's insulted position as bastard. Any liberal-minded member of the audience will sympathize with his position, will they not? especially nowadays. We are not in favour of things like queer-bashing, of anti-Semitism, so Edmund's argument 'Why bastard? wherefore base?' is put from his own viewpoint, and it is eminently reasonable. If it has made him a little violent in his outrage, well, he has had provocation – so a liberal might argue.

The skill of Shakespeare's craft here is in blending the elements in the speech: the doctrine; the conventional villainy; the psychological portrayal through the way the verse is shaped of a mind in motion. As a dramatist he has to show Edmund from his own point of view, though he must also control that point of view within his total structure. Add to this the further potential of sexual attractiveness and villainy (and the villainy may even heighten the sexuality), and one begins to see the enormous richness which the writer offers to the player.

Beckett's method is substantially different. Direct audience address is not permitted (which made us conspiratorial with Edmund). The naturalistic style of Beckett does not permit Krapp even to talk to himself and thus reveal his memories. How important, too, that sense of memory is. It is all recollection, whereas Edmund lives in the present. He springs at us fully formed. Krapp has declined to his present position over a long period. What we hear is an address, some years ago, to the tape recorder which now repeats those past words to Krapp, who listens in silence, while we, as it were, overhear in silence also. Human inter-relation through dialogue is broken. Krapp spoke then only to a machine. Now he does not speak. What is recorded upon the machine, appropriately, describes the breakdown of a relationship. The scene is one of the most potent evocations of loneliness that exist in theatre.

Consider the pauses. The importance of silence was raised in the first chapter. Compare Edmund. He crowds his speech with words. The thought runs on so rapidly there is, as it were, no time to think. Each of those pauses in the tape demands that we think. What was it that Krapp thought then? What does he think now? The living presence of the old man (close to death) does not tell us as he listens to his former life. At one point his lips move – but no words emerge. Pause follows pause. Anyone who has followed the advice to voice the scene will understand at once the importance of the orchestration of those pauses. How long should the silence be? The process is climatic. At the very end the tape runs on in silence, and Krapp, quite motionless, sits silent before it. How long, in stage time, does that final silence endure – and how long in imaginative time? For eternity, I suggest. The title tells us there will be no more tapes. There is no more for the old man to say.

The technique of the craftsman here is to make us creative. By imagining what it is that Krapp remembers we are induced to think as if we were Krapp. It is what is called empathy. The potentiality is therefore enormous, although shaped by the rhetoric. 'Perhaps my best years are gone', the voice on the tape says. 'When there was a chance of happiness. But I wouldn't want them back. Not with the fire in me now. No, I wouldn't want them back.' That statement is asking a question. Despite what the tape says, does the old man now want middle-age back again, so that he might come again by the same processes to where he is now? Does he, or does he not? To be, or not to be, that is the question. It is not answered.

Considered thus Krapp, like Edmund, acquires a moral dimension. The character is revealed not just for the sake of character. It is our fate as human beings which we empathetically imagine in becoming Krapp. The poetic and symbolic dimensions of the scene add to its potentialities – remember the white light in darkness. See the reel upon the tape spinning and spinning in silence. Hear the implications of 'We lay there without moving. But under us all moved, and moved us'. Just as much as Edmund's speech this character tells us something of the nature of Nature. Add to this merely one more dimension, that the speech is both tragic, and *comic* – 'gooseberries, she said' – and that the speaking voice must embrace both potentialities, and enough has been said to reveal the range of the craft. We say nothing about character if we view it merely as character.

Most characters in plays reveal themselves through physical interaction and dialogue with other characters. It was easier to start with monologue, but unrepresentative. Because plays concern inter-relationship character analysis is bogus just for its own sake in isolation. You cannot discuss the part without seeing the whole. (Even long extracts are therefore imperfect.) Let us stay with plays already considered. Examine the way Edmund is first introduced at the beginning of *Lear*, and our first sight of the Boyle family in *Juno and the Paycock*. In Shakespeare, Gloucester, Edmund's father, and Kent are discussing the king's decision to divide the kingdom. Kent then notices Edmund. In O'Casey Mary, making up at the kitchen table, is reading about the contemporary civil war in Ireland. Johnny, who has one arm, is sitting before the fire.

Kent	Is not this your son, my lord?
Gloucester	His breeding, sir, hath been at my charge: I have so often blushed to acknowledge him, that now I am brazed to it.
Kent	I cannot conceive you.
Gloucester	Sir, this young fellow's mother could; whereupon she grew round-wombed, and had, indeed, sir, a son for her cradle ere she had a husband for her bed. Do you smell a fault?
Kent	I cannot wish the fault undone, the issue of it being so proper.
Gloucester	But I have a son, sir, by order of law, some year elder than this, who yet is no dearer in my account: though this knave came somewhat saucily into the world before he was sent for, yet was his mother fair; there was good sport at his making, and the whoreson must be acknowledged. Do you know this noble gentleman, Edmund?
Edmund	No, my lord.
Gloucester	My Lord of Kent: remember him hereafter as my honourable friend.
Edmund	My services to your lordship.
Kent	I must love you, and sue to know you better.
Edmund	Sir, I shall study deserving.
Gloucester	He hath been out nine years, and away he shall again. The king is coming.

Mrs Boyle	Isn't he come in yet?
Mary	No, mother.
Mrs Boyle	(*R*) Oh, he'll come in when he likes; strutting about the town like a paycock with Joxer, I suppose. (*She puts the parcel on the table*) I hear all about Mrs Tancred's son is in this morning's paper. (*She crosses behind Mary, takes off her hat and black shawl, and flings them on the bed in the alcove*)
Mary	The full details are in it this mornin'; seven wounds he had – one entherin' the neck, with an exit wound beneath the left shoulder-blade; another in the left breast penethratin' the heart, an'. . .
Johnny	(*springing up from the fire*) Oh, quit that readin', for God's

	sake! Are yous losin' all your feelin's? It'll soon be that none of yous'll read anythin' that's not about butcherin'!
	(*Johnny goes quickly into the room L*)
Mary	(*looking after Johnny*) He's getting very sensitive, all of a sudden.
	(*Mrs Boyle comes down to the table R*)
Mrs Boyle	I'll read it myself, Mary, by an' by, when I come home. Everybody's sayin' that he was a Die-hard – thanks be to God that Johnny had nothin' to do with him this long time. . . (*She opens the parcel and takes out some sausages, which she places on a plate*) Ah, then, if that father o' yours doesn't come in soon for his breakfast, he may go without any; I'll not wait much longer for him. (*She takes the plate of sausages from the table, goes over to the dresser, and puts them in the bottom cupboard*)
Mary	Can't you let him get it himself when he comes in?
Mrs Boyle	Yes, an' let him bring in Joxer Daly along with him? Ay, that's what he'd like, an' that's what he's waitin' for – till he thinks I'm gone to work, an' then sail in with the boul' Joxer, to burn all the coal an' dhrink all the tea in the place, to show them what a good Samaritan he is! But I'll stop here till he comes in, if I have to wait till tomorrow mornin'. (*She goes over and sits beside the fire*)

In approaching character we must not forget basics: the use of stage space, the appearance and action of the players. Shakespeare has divided his empty space into two areas. In one Kent and Gloucester have been discussing affairs of state. These are important matters and hold our attention. Separated from them is Edmund, who is neither involved in the action nor speech. Who is he? What is his function here? Kent and Gloucester are middle-aged and important courtiers – territorial magnates. Edmund is a young man returned from abroad (and we shall learn) without land. Age and costume are therefore different. (Marlowe uses a parallel device at the beginning of *Edward II*, already instanced.)

At once, therefore, Shakespeare has divided his actors (as England is to be divided by the king). Edmund is alienated from his father and his society by the use of the stage space, his age, his dress. The entire scene is down key – prose rather than verse. The most obvious reason is to distinguish this, as

prologue, from the commencement of the main action: the
entry of Lear. But it works also in exactly the same way as a
low-key prologue for Edmund. The next time we see him he is
alone, and his first major speech is the monologue already
considered: 'Thou, Nature, art my goddess.' Until then he has
only said 'No, my lord', and 'Sir, I shall study deserving.' First
mere social phrases – each expressive of subservient status:
'my lord', 'sir' – then the explosion as the man behind the
social phrases is revealed in the big speech later.

The development is a surprise, but once it is made one
observes the connection. The subservient character rebels; the
individual who is socially alienated searches for social status.
In comparing the major monologue with Beckett it was argued
that Shakespeare crowds the playing time with words – as if a
pent up torrent were bursting forth – whereas Beckett uses
silence, and stretches the pauses to even greater length as the
dying Krapp finds nothing more worth saying about life. That
is not to claim that Shakespeare does not know how to use
silence, or pauses. Here the silence of Edmund is as significant
as that, for instance, of Pegeen Mike blowing the sod at the fire
in *The Playboy*. The technique is imaginative empathy. What
must Edmund be thinking and feeling (the sub-text) as Gloucester makes a series of coarse (and are they embarrassed?)
jokes out of his bastardy: the pun upon conceived; the embarrassing 'Do you smell a fault?' the descriptions 'knave',
'saucily', 'the whoreson must be acknowledged'. One notes
how Gloucester at once compares the 'whoreson' whom he has
to acknowledge with 'legitimate Edgar': 'But I have a son, sir
by order of *law*, some year elder than this, who yet is no dearer
in my account'.

This raises the question of Gloucester's character. That is not
our topic. But the imagined internal reaction of Edmund to
Gloucester's description of him is dependent on how we interpret the tone of that description. When Gloucester says
Edmund is 'dear' to him, does he say it because it is the proper
sentiment to express, but he does not mean it? Kent, perhaps,
feels that Gloucester is embarrassing Edmund, so he goes out
of his way to compliment the young man: 'I cannot wish the
fault undone, the issue of it being so proper' (i.e. what a hand-
some young man your son is – but that could be a form of
words only). There is a difference between the embarrassment
a son feels at the jocular vulgarity of an affectionate father, and

the antagonism which hostility and exclusion might create. Which is it? 'He hath been out [i.e. abroad] nine years, and away he shall again', says Gloucester. Is that to be as 'dear' as lawful Edgar? In short, the deductions we might draw as to what Edmund thinks and feels depend on what Gloucester feels and says, which are themselves open to more than one interpretation. The scene, which is a simple one, has more than one potential reading, and how we interpret Edmund's character depends on how we interpret Gloucester's, Kent's (in the polite remark) and the entire situation. Thus the character, as individual, cannot be separated from the relative position in which he is placed. Nor can we be certain that any interpretation we give to his silences here is the correct one.

The scene is not there just to show character, or even just to advance the plot. Thematic concerns emerge: law, Edmund as 'natural' son; and conventional criteria apply: the bastard as villain. Later it is said in the play that Gloucester's blinding is a punishment for his sexual fault. It would be wrong to separate character from these concerns, but part of the situation is the demand that we interpret the scene *as if* the characters were real. Fifty years ago that would not need to be said. Nowadays some academic critics would deny it.

O'Casey's psychological naturalism is more strongly emphasized by the kind of set in which his characters move. This is Ireland, 1922 – we have Mary's interest in the report of the civil war in the newspaper. By comparison one may see that the *as if* in Shakespeare is less related to a particular time and place. *King Lear* could be Jacobean, or any time in history. The mythic nature of the situation, the dividing of Lear's kingdom, is more apparent compared with the particular event of the dividing of Ireland in 1922. Edmund is both a man we can understand as if he were real, and representative of something typical, even 'eternal'. The Boyles seem more local.

Granted these basic differences in theatrical convention there is, none the less, in O'Casey a blending of the general with the particular. Thus we may read the separation of the Boyles in the room as itself indicative of the division of the family. Each is wrapped up in a personal little sphere: Johnny at the fire; Mary who is reading the paper and arranging her hair (she is about to meet her boyfriend); Mrs Boyle worn down by caring for the family, and at this moment preparing the breakfast. The naturalistic set imposes upon the players a busyness of action in comparison with which Shakespeare's characters may appear hieratic and remote, but each action communicates a larger meaning. Mary is the family intellectual (she is reading), but what she reads creates the atmosphere of war which surrounds the family. At this moment it is just so many words for each of them – 'I'll read it myself, Mary, by an' by, when I come home' (how often we treat newspaper disasters that way), but when Johnny himself is killed at the end Mrs Boyle will learn by experience to feel and judge what at this moment is a distraction from laying Captain Boyle's breakfast. Johnny will represent all sons killed in war.

Johnny's reaction, on the other hand, is exaggerated – and taken with indifference. We ask why it is the one-armed young man acts in this way, we note how little effect this has upon the others. Is he always like this? Why do they not bother about him? The act of leaving the family fireside, too, indicates his separation from the family (compare Edmund's alienation from Gloucester). At the centre of the action Mrs Boyle's preoccupation with breakfast – she is the only person doing anything for the family – tells us not only of her character, but her pivotal role as the person who holds together the divided household.

Therefore, just as in Shakespeare, there is a blending of the psychological emphasis – we judge the words and actions of these people *as if* they were real – with larger thematic concerns. It is a question at any moment of where we place the emphasis. Here, most probably, on first reading simply on learning what these people are like and on the plot. The other matters are overtones. We are right to read it in that order: first the people. The long character description of Mrs Boyle which O'Casey gives immediately prior to this scene reads as if it were from a nineteenth-century novel. He is controlling our reaction to the character, and pointing the interpretation of the actor, far more closely than Shakespeare. Likewise the short episode with its constant references to Captain Boyle – 'Isn't he come in yet?' and so on – is building our expectation for the entry of the principal character, and filling in information about him: he struts like a peacock, he is late for his breakfast (has he no job then?), he is extravagant, he pretends to be a Samaritan by dispensing profusely what others have earned. All the thrust of the writing is upon building up a pre-portrait of the Captain. Only when we step back from the picture may the larger issues reveal themselves. Boyle's giant follies mirror the folly of Ireland herself, obsessed with her own importance, a nation of worthless braggarts. He is a huge, humour character of traditional comedy such as Jonson, Molière, Dickens might create. (For Jonson, see p.75.)

Thus, just as with Shakespeare, diverse elements combine to provide the medium in which the character moves, and may potentially develop. One must grasp that context. When we talk about character in drama we violate the work the playwright has done in putting things together if we do not see the function of the role in the structure as a whole; the way different levels of the text operate simultaneously; what kind of conventions determine the way characters speak and move. Gertrude's speech on Ophelia's drowning would mean something quite different if said by Mrs Boyle about Mrs Tancred's son in *Juno* – even the very fact of it being in verse would signify differently. A specific date for Edmund's attack on legitimacy would give his outburst about Edgar a specific political dimension in *Lear* which, out of time and place, it does not possess. This has nothing to do with the old, facile, distinction between 'flat' and 'round' characters. It is a question of convention and function, not of 'type' and 'real person'. What are the formal devices of this particular kind of play; in what kinds of way are characters created, used, *developed* within that particular kind of structure? These examples only scratch the surface. One must read, and compare, and again and again. Only that way will the similarities, and differences, of the craftsman's creations emerge.

5 'The Message'

It is an old saying that the aim of art is 'to instruct by pleasing'. Sometimes, to indicate the traditional nature of the view, it is said that writers mix the *utile* with the *dulce* (the words are those of the Latin poet Horace, who was not accustomed to say new things). In our own age the vigorous Marxist propagandist Bertolt Brecht, though he called some of his plays *teaching* pieces, also declared that we go to the theatre to have *fun*. (His ideas sound grander in German.) Charlie Chaplin was one of Brecht's heroes. A piece of comic and popular cinema theatre like *Modern Times* has a strong message. We do plays wrong to separate their message from the pleasure we receive from them. But, to discuss ideology with brevity, in what follows the concentration is upon the moral.

Least need be said here on plays which clearly state their message, as if it were written up like a slogan on a wall. The morality plays of the medieval Christian Church were a means by which institutionalized religion would teach through popular embodiment in action, before your very eyes, the precepts of Christianity (to audiences in part illiterate, and impoverished in vocabulary). The same is true of the miracle plays on the Bible story, when the Bible was in Latin. They taught how Christ died to redeem the sin of Adam, how the Old Testament was fulfilled in the New, how there will be a judgement which will separate those saved by God's grace from the wicked and the damned. Such ideas run deep into the theatre of the Shakespearian age. In *The Merchant of Venice* Shylock, with his insistence on 'the law' speaks as a Jew of the Old Testament, Portia, with her insistence on 'mercy' as a Christian of the New Testament; and there is a judgement. It would be a gross act of reduction to explain *The Merchant of Venice* merely in those terms, but the tradition is strongly present.

Likewise, in our own days, Marxist ideology has provided a strong framework of ideas and a drama of strong political commitment. The exploitation of the working classes is an act of violence by the bourgeoisie. Provoke the bourgeoisie into revealing that violence and the masses will be politically instructed. The revolution will be advanced. Such ideas, in a pluralist society like Britain today, do not have the quality of collective social affirmation which the performance of a miracle cycle of plays would have at medieval Chester or York. In Soviet society they have. Meyerhold records a performance in Russia of Verhaeren's *The Dawn* which tells of the transformation of 'a capitalist war into an international uprising'. The first performance took place on the third anniversary of the October revolution, 7 November 1920, and the walls were hung with political slogans. Civil war was still continuing between the Whites and the Reds. At a certain point in the play a Herald entered to deliver a bulletin on the progress of the real war. One night Meyerhold's 'highest aspirations' were fulfilled when the Herald announced a decisive Soviet victory at Perekop 'and the entire theatre rose in a triumphant rendering of the "Internationale".'

Theatre has often fulfilled this kind of ideological function in society, although not often so spectacularly. This effectiveness clearly relates to its nature as a public act in the presence of an audience who are involved collectively in the experience. It is frequently said by those who wish to affirm the importance of art that this is a kind of ritual – a repetition formally of symbolic acts by which societies declare their identity and shape their future. There is certainly an analogy, although to claim a performance of *Hamlet* is equivalent to the Mass in the Roman Catholic Church seems to me highly dubious. None the less, the experience of theatre is one way people declare their common relationship. Martin Esslin in *An Anatomy of Drama* cites the patriotic speeches of *Henry V* as an example, and certainly Olivier's film of the play in the Second World War had an important function to perform in Britain. I suspect that the role of Tommy Handley in the radio comedy series ITMA was greater. In our present society perhaps the major piece of 'ritual' theatre is *Coronation Street,* the most popular of television dramas.

That very name 'Coronation Street' makes an affirmation. It is not 'Stanlinallee' or 'Clement Attlee Gardens'. It suggests that the everyday folk of Britain are united in a common affection for their royal family. That tight little community of north-country characters reflects still the continuing British ideal of the happy village carried now into the industrial world. Consider the name of the pub: 'The Rover's Return'. Folk grumble about their narrow lot in the Street, but this is where their heart is. If they go away, this is to where the rover would wish to return. Although the setting is now an industrial village, it is not an eighties council estate. These are Victorian houses in the street, reflecting a conservative nostalgia for an age when, if we know people had it tough, yet Britain was a great nation. It was also a nation of white people. The Pakistanis and West Indians have not moved in on this street. The sturdy folk own their property, and work in small enterprises on a person-to-person basis. To speak to its mass audience *Coronation Street* either avoids all major issues of controversy or viewpoints are carefully balanced: there are no race riots, Marxist demagogues, abrasive feminists in the Street – extremism is not the British way. The pub, in particular, binds the community. How changed this is from the ideology of the morality play where the tavern was the place where Gluttony and Lechery might lure Idle Youth to Satan (a pattern Shakespeare suggests with Falstaff and Hal). Now beer bonds the British. Why? Look at the advertisements. How much of the money is coming from the breweries? Look too at our social customs. The local pub is a peculiarly British institution. We boast of it to foreigners.

Coronation Street is held by some to be classic theatre. It is a view I share. What Dickens is to Victorian England, the Street is now. We cannot separate our reading of Dickens, or medieval plays, or Brecht – what we call 'literature' – from the theatre that is round us every day. It is a fault of this study freely acknowledged (as Martin Esslin too confesses) that in present-day education theatre means written play texts for playhouses. But most theatre today is television and cinema.

Although all works of art with ideological content appeal for an affirmation from their audience – witness, in general, the happy endings of comedies in the institution of marriage 'betokening concord' – not all audiences are united in their outlook. *The Playboy* was shouted down. A recent work by Howard Brenton, *The Romans in Britain*, performed at the National Theatre, likened the English army in Northern Ireland

to the Roman occupation of Celtic Britain, and portrayed a
Roman soldier homosexually raping a native. Strong objection
was raised to the scene. It is fashionable to claim that such
moves to censor are illiberal or philistine. Perhaps. But the
philosopher Plato roused similar objections. You cannot have
it both ways: if ideological plays are ritual affirmations of a
collective social view, societies quite rightly will reject rituals
which challenge their deeply held values.

This analogy with ritual is important, but it does not hold (I
suggest) for many of the great works of theatre. Stanislavski's
as if is closer to the mark. Plays are creations of the imagination in which the writer works out a situation with characters:
like a scenario. If the king were to abdicate and to divide his
country between three daughters (for he has no son to inherit),
what might be likely to happen given the mixture of good and
evil which we see in the world? That is the *as if* situation of *King
Lear*. In this kind of play instruction comes not by telling
us moral messages directly – although moral things are often
stated directly – but is analogous to the way we learn about
the world generally. We have to imagine situations in plays, or
real life – if I go for that job interview, what is likely to happen
at the interview; if I get that job what will it be like? So theatre
is also like the games that children play, which we know are
essential to learning. Lion cubs play at hunting before they
have to hunt to live.

The play is more complex than this, however, in so far as it is
a work of art. It has conventions it must follow; it must work
things out according to the proper (and indefinable) logic of its
internal laws of creative force. You can make many kinds of
wheel – but a three-sided wheel will not do for locomotion.
Muss es sein? asked Beethoven working upon a theme: must it
be? and then wrote, *es muss sein*: it must be. That is the logic of
the development of this piece of craft. In particular, in many
works of theatre it is clear that the artist essentially has
accepted that each character within the piece must see that
piece from their own point of view and possess their own
integrity. The ideologically committed will object to that claim
as being merely liberal – how can a good Marxist show a good
capitalist, for all capitalists are either knaves or fools; how can
a good Christian allow virtue to the race that crucified Christ?
To which all one can reply is that the laws of drama have made
demands which frequently challenge the ideology of state or

religion. It is not for this little book to determine correct political or religious readings of theatre.

The kind of thing which happens when a playwright dramatizes even the opposition may be represented by a speech such as this by Marlowe's Mephostophiles in the morality play *Dr Faustus*. (The devil, in the tradition, is without question evil.) Faustus jests that hell is a fable. The evil one replies:

Why, this is hell, nor am I out of it.
Think'st thou that I, who saw the face of God
And tasted the eternal joys of heaven,
Am not tormented with ten thousand hells
In being depriv'd of everlasting bliss?
O Faustus, leave these frivolous demands,
Which strike a terror to my fainting soul.

(III.78–84)

Historical record tells us that Marlowe was considered a blasphemer by part of his audience. One may see why. For perhaps the first time in drama the devil speaks from his own point of view, and we see his lot as tragic. The evil spirit laments, and laments in the most solemn language, the unhappiness of his position separated from everlasting bliss. Cannot Faustus appreciate that to the soul without God this world itself is hell? This warning does not come from a clergyman (though with brilliant irony Marlowe has dressed the devil like a cleric, though as a *Roman Catholic* friar for a *Protestant* audience) – it comes from the one character in the play who so far has experiential knowledge of hell. Therefore the devil exhorts Faustus, and with complete seriousness, not to go on. What Faustus is about is 'frivolous' (extraordinary word), and terrifies the devil so much that his very soul faints. That is why Marlowe so deeply disturbed his audience and is a better dramatist than a mere clerical propagandist like Ulpian Fulwell. We feel the pain of Mephostophiles as tragic; we feel the terrible nature of his separation from God, which he laments. What kind of Creator is it, therefore, that treats his creation in this manner? 'See, see where Christ's blood streams in the firmament', cries Faustus later, separated too from everlasting bliss. What kind of God has asked for redemption by blood sacrifice? It strikes terror to the fainting soul.

The ideology of plays frequently is constructed from tensions of this kind, and the 'message' of the play exists in that state of tension, not in particular moral labels which may be extracted from the text. The clumsy critic digs out a slogan. Consider Irena's 'I'll go on working and working!' from Chekhov's *The Three Sisters*. Taken as Chekhov's 'message' it turns the dramatist into a proto-Marxist critic of a decadent, lazy, land-owning society – or consider Edgar's 'The Gods are just' from *King Lear* which might be used to recruit Shakespeare as a Christian optimist. But it is like extracting the role of a trombone from a symphonic score and saying *that* is what the symphony is about. Instead, we must learn to hear the entire orchestra, and not just at one moment, but through the total experience as it is shaped in time.

At the end of *Juno and the Paycock*, Mrs Boyle delivers one of the most deeply felt attacks upon war in English theatre. She has learnt experientially from the murder (justified judicial execution, the republicans would say) of her son Johnny, and she recalls, word for word, an earlier speech of Mrs Tancred whose son had died on the other side (it is his death Mary was reading from the paper at the beginning of the play):

Ah, why didn't I remember that then he wasn't a Diehard or a Stater, but only a poor dead son! It's well I remember all that she said – an' it's my turn to say it now: What was the pain I suffered, Johnny, bringin' you into the world to carry you to your cradle, to the pains I'll suffer carryin' you out o' the world to bring you to your grave! Mother o' God, Mother o' God, have pity on us all!. . . Sacred Heart o' Jesus, take away our hearts o' stone, and give us hearts o' flesh! Take away this murdherin' hate, an' give us Thine own eternal love!

A lesser dramatist would have dropped the curtain there on this message. After Mrs Boyle goes out O'Casey does not close the scene, however, though the audience must naturally feel that this overwhelming speech and its powerful moral demands the final curtain. (Let us recollect, too, that this was delivered to an audience who had just gone through that civil war.) Instead, after a long pause – whatever pause, like that in Beckett's play, is right – Captain Boyle and his side-kick Joxer reel in drunk and end the play with a comic scene:

Boyle   The counthry'll have to steady itself. . . it's goin'. . . to hell . . . Where'r all. . . the chairs. . . gone to. . . steady itself,

> Joxer. . . Chairs'll. . . have to. . . steady themselves. . . No
> matther. . . what any one may. . . say. . . Irelan' sober. . . is
> Irelan'. . . free.
>
> *Joxer* (*stretching himself on the bed*) Chains. . . an'. . .
> slaveree. . . that's a darlin' motto. . . a daaarlin'. . . motto!

That comic resolution is compelled by artistic necessity. Anyone who will play the last act of *Juno* will realize that Mrs
Boyle's curtain speech is fine, but O'Casey's resolution is finer.
The artistic reason is that the play is a tragi-comedy, and as
such both voices *must* speak at the end, or the orchestral forces
would be unbalanced. Nothing is irrelevant. Even in brief
extract, from which most emotional feeling has been lost, it is
apparent how relevant to the theme of the play the comic
speeches are. (In a famous phrase Boyle gives the true curtain
line: 'th' whole worl's. . . in a terr. . . ible state o'. . . chassis!'.)
O'Casey is using the same dramatic technique as Shakespeare
uses with the porter in *Macbeth*. But it is essential to join the
comedy to the thematic message, and to set this comedy
against Mrs Boyle's tragedy. She has learnt one thing, Boyle
has learnt nothing, but his world, just as much as hers, goes on.
It is an experiential fact, and the audience are taken through
the experience. When we wished to weep – indeed may have
wept – we are made to laugh, and we might argue that the
capacity to laugh, even when death is all around, is as important a 'message' as to protest against the dying of the light. But
how crude it is to use that kind of formulation to describe the
relation of the parts which give even *pleasure* in our apprecia-
tion of the perfect working out of the artistic problem of the
ending.

The importance of orchestration, the essential requirement
that we see the whole, makes it even more difficult in this
chapter to illustrate by extract. One needs the entire play to
perceive the balance of the forces within it, and as the chapter
on genre has indicated, even a play in its entirety is insufficient
for we need to appreciate the working out of conventions
which may be affirmed or challenged. With that proviso, a
simple illustration may be made using the first of Marlowe's
two plays entitled *Tamburlaine*. Take almost any speech of the
protagonist (main character) and he blasphemes against what
has been described as the Elizabethan world picture: he rebels
against princes, he tells us that God (Jove) himself was a rebel,

he threatens to chase God out of heaven, he tells us war (not love) moves the universe, that it is not so glorious to be in heaven as to reign on earth, he challenges the wheel of Fortune (which everyone knows goes round):

I hold the Fates bound fast in iron chains,
And with my hand turn Fortune's wheel about,
And sooner shall the sun fall from his sphere
Than Tamburlaine be slain or overcome.

(I.ii.173–6)

For three hours we wait for this 'villain' to get his come-uppance – which everyone in the play warns us he will get (*cf. Richard III*). But he wins every battle. He kills all his enemies (sometimes horribly). He marries the most beautiful woman in the play. Then, immensely rich, powerful and feared, he announces a truce, and retires to the city of Samarkand where history tells us, he lived to an immense old age. What do we make of that? We thought we were watching a morality play, and then we get just the opposite resolution from that we expected. One must see the play as a whole, therefore, and cannot extract speeches. Conventional morality, and dramatic (and historic) fact are brought into collision. The villain triumphs. 'Applaud his fortunes as you please' the Prologue states. We are left to work out our response depending on what sort of people we are.

Debate, therefore, is often built into the way dramatists explore ideas. Different viewpoints are brought into relation, and the dramatic debate carries over from play world to real world. The major examples for this chapter are from Ibsen's *A Doll's House* (1878–9) (one of Mary Boyle's books) and Congreve's *The Way of the World* (1700). Both concern the *Trafford Tanzi* theme, woman's liberty. In Ibsen Nora has acted the part of a 'doll' wife to Torvald Helmer – she is a pretty chattel with which he plays – but at the end of the action she resolves to leave her family to educate herself (I suppress the intricacies of the plot which concern financial dependence and deceits). In Congreve the beautiful, witty, coquettish Millamant, who has fallen head over heels in love with the rake-hero, Mirabell, is about to agree to be his wife. She wants both her 'will and pleasure' *and* marriage.

Nora	Listen, Torvald. I have heard that when a wife deserts her husband's house, as I am doing now, he is legally freed from all obligations towards her. In any case I set you free from all your obligations. You are not to feel yourself bound in the slightest way, any more than I shall. There must be perfect freedom on both sides. See, here is your ring back. Give me mine.
Helmer	That too?
Nora	That too.
Helmer	Here it is.
Nora	That's right. Now it is all over. I have put the keys here. The maids know all about everything in the house – better than I do. Tomorrow, after I have left her, Christine will come here and pack up my own things that I brought with me from home. I will have them sent after me.
Helmer	All over! All over! – Nora, shall you never think of me again?
Nora	I know I shall often think of you and the children and this house.
Helmer	May I write to you, Nora?
Nora	No – never. You must not do that.
Helmer	But at least let me send you –
Nora	Nothing – nothing –
Helmer	Let me help you if you are in want.
Nora	No. I can receive nothing from a stranger.
Helmer	Nora – can I never be anything more than a stranger to you?
Nora	(*taking her bag*). Ah, Torvald, the most wonderful thing of all would have to happen.
Helmer	Tell me what that would be!
Nora	Both you and I would have to be so changed that – Oh, Torvald, I don't believe any longer in wonderful things happening.
Helmer	But I will believe in it. Tell me. So changed that –?
Nora	That our life together would be a real wedlock. Good-bye. (*She goes out through the hall.*)
Helmer	(*sinks down on a chair at the door and buries his face in*

his hands). Nora! Nora! (*Looks round, and rises.*) Empty. She is gone. (*A hope flashes across his mind.*) The most wonderful thing of all –?(*The sound of a door shutting is heard from below.*)

CURTAIN

Millamant	My dear Liberty, shall I leave thee? My faithful Solitude, my darling Contemplation, must I bid you then adieu? Ay-h adieu! My Morning Thoughts, agreeable Wakings, indolent Slumbers, all ye *douceurs*, ye *Sommeils du Matin*, adieu! – I can't do it! 'Tis more than impossible! – Positively, Mirabell, I'll lie a-bed in a morning as long as I please.
Mirabell	Then I'll get up in a morning as early as I please.
Millamant	Ah! Idle creature, get up when you will! And, d'ye hear, I won't be called names after I'm married. Positively, I won't be called names.
Mirabell	Names!
Millamant	Aye. As wife, spouse, my dear, joy, jewel, love, sweetheart, and the rest of that nauseous cant, in which men and their wives are so fulsomely familiar. I shall never bear that. Good Mirabell, don't let us be familiar or fond, nor kiss before folks, like my Lady Fadler and Sir Francis; nor go to Hyde Park together the first Sunday in a new chariot to provoke eyes and whispers, and then never be seen there together again; as if we were proud of one another the first week, and ashamed of one another ever after. Let us never visit together, nor go to a play together, but let us be very strange and well bred. Let us be as strange as if we had been married a great while, and as well bred as if we were not married at all.
Mirabell	Have you any more conditions to offer? Hitherto your demands are pretty reasonable.
Millamant	Trifles. As liberty to pay and receive visits to and from whom I please; to write and receive letters without interrogatories or wry faces on your part; to wear what I please, and choose conversation with regard only to my own taste; to have no obligation upon me to converse with wits that I don't like, because they are your acquaintance, or to be intimate with fools because they may be

your relations; come to dinner when I please, dine in my dressing-room when I'm out of humour, without giving a reason; to have my closet inviolate; to be sole empress of my tea table, which you must never presume to approach without first asking leave; and lastly, where-ever I am, you shall always knock at the door before you come in. These articles subscribed, if I continue to endure you a little longer, I may by degrees dwindle into a wife.

(IV.v.)

Before discussing Ibsen's meaning let us not forget the basic matters this study has raised. The scene is built round significant action – especially the return of the rings, the shutting of the inner, and then the outer doors. The set is nineteenth-century naturalistic, and, therefore, for many of Ibsen's audience a matter of here and now concern: 'these are people like us: these are the kind of problems we face'. The characters act as if real, but also represent typically 'husband' and 'wife', or, at least, 'husband and wife in nineteenth-century middle-class society'. Those who know the whole play will be aware of the personal intricacies of their relationship and the individual quality of the characters will have a larger share in the reader's consciousness. This cannot be supplied here, and the typical element – husband and wife – is more prominent. All moves to the climactic event, the shutting of the house door.

How do we interpret that event? The dramatist refuses to spell out the whole meaning, passing on the problem to us (this kind of play is sometimes labelled generically a 'problem' play). A feminist interpretation might be that Helmer was wrong to treat his wife as a doll and a chattel (and great sympathy for her is moved by the plot). A woman has a right to her independence. Good on you, sister, you walk out on the man and stand on your own feet!

But is the text saying that, or is it the feminist? The text repeats three times the phrase 'wonderful thing'. If Nora and Helmer were 'changed' that would be a wonderful thing. There would be 'real wedlock' between them. She says then she wants marriage, if it is 'real'. But she believes no longer. He too, at the end, has a flash of hope – as if he sees in himself the capacity for change – and, at that very moment of hope, the door slams. Hope and despair unite in the man at the same instant. Does a way forward exist for men and women to 'real' marriage – or does the door always slam upon our expectation? What, indeed, might 'real marriage' be? Not this, certainly. Then what? That exchange of rings – is it a sign of the end of all marriage? We end in despair?

Do we all approve of Nora? Walking out on a husband and children – is that a way to find 'real' marriage, or simply a refusal of responsibility? There are many married couples, struggling from day to day with their relation, who might well say they must compromise with unhappiness for the sake of the family. What will happen to the home and the children when the mother has gone? What will happen to Nora? She has got to find a job – no easy task then as now – and are there not losses in living alone and being tied to a job, just as one might be tied to a home? It is often said that characters do not live outside their play worlds. It all depends upon what kind of play. This work demands that we ask questions about what happens later. Artistically it is brought to a fine resolution by that slamming of the door – at once our own argument begins. What is the answer to all these questions above?

Congreve, on the other hand, is giving a future wife's description of a 'real marriage'. This is comedy, and the generic convention is that hero and heroine wed, and live happily ever after. Millamant goes beyond the conventions – walks through the door like Nora as it were! – by spelling out what living happily ever after entails for her. The first thing we note is that it involves initially the surrender of that very liberty which Nora has gone in search of. 'My dear Liberty, shall I leave thee?'

It has been written of this scene that it expresses Congreve's ideal of marriage, even that the ideal is derived from the views of the contemporary philosopher Locke upon society as founded upon contract. If this little book has had any success it is to be hoped that the reader is not exploring the dialogue in that way, but asking rather questions like, in what way do the generic conventions of comedy affect what is being said? In what way has the playwright constructed his protagonist? Even, how does setting this upon a platform stage (rather than Helmer's sitting room) affect the relation of the characters?

Let us take the question of the comedy first. 'My dear Liberty, shall I leave thee?' she asks – a serious question – yet, at the end of the speech declares 'Positively, Mirabell, I'll lie a-bed in a morning as long as I please'. The juxtaposition of the big question and the trivial conclusion is rhetorically a device called bathos, and is (I hope) found comic. But it raises questions just as problematical as Ibsen's. One way of looking at the character here is that she is an affected coquette, a variant of the comic type of woman as *varium et mutabile* – a changeable thing – and one whose inconsequential mind, leaping from liberty to lying in late, shows too how trivial women are. Bed, tea table, riding in a coach in the park – that is what upper-class girls in 1700 saw as marriage. It is both funny and satirical.

Such a reading of the message seems a betrayal of one's ear for style, however. This discourse is so articulately witty, so breathlessly loaded (try speaking it!) that it sounds extremely intelligent. (Try to judge the *tone*.) Nora's speech is puddingish in comparison, not very bright. Admittedly everyone talks cleverly in this kind of comedy (*cf*. Wilde, Shaw, or the great original Jonson). But the cleverness of the dialogue *is* a sign of intelligence. There is a strong case for saying that Millamant herself is turning into wit matters which if treated seriously would stop her marrying at all. Therefore she has to joke. There are some things in human relationships so bad that we have to see their funny side if we are to find happiness: 'and then never be seen. . . together again; as if we were proud of one another the first week, and ashamed of one another ever after'. That is good comedy, because it is close to tragedy, and she is advancing the paradox that the only basis for happy marriage is for the partners to behave as if they were unmarried – not in the literal sense of staying apart, but by continuing honest courtship into marriage: 'I won't be called names. . . . As wife, spouse, my dear, joy, jewel, love, sweet-heart, and the rest of that nauseous cant'. We laugh, I guess, because of painful recognition, and the laughter wins support for Millamant's viewpoint.

It is not 'ideal' marriage so much as an attempt to find a way of avoiding all the ills of marriage to which love, none the less, and social necessity drive men and women. But what of the last, long speech? 'Trifles', she says: but by now we ought to be sufficiently alert never to believe directly what she says, for if 'liberty' were initially reduced to a trifle – lying in bed late – conversely the trifles here provide a means of turning liberty into libertinism: I will choose my own friends, and see whom I like, when I like, and be alone when I like: 'And lastly, where-ever I am, you shall always knock at the door before you come in'. That social custom – marriage is formal politeness – is the kind of thing which has suggested the phrase 'comedy of manners' as apt description of Congreve's craft. But it is not just manners. What might a wife be doing alone with a friend that a husband must knock before he comes in? Having an affair?

Again, it is not said directly. The comic mode makes the serious thing a joke, and passes obliquely by what will not be directly verbalized. Compare the direct way Ibsen batters at his 'wonderful thing'. That obliqueness in Congreve is now close to deceit. If liberty is necessary in marriage between equal partners, at what point does it become so great that there is no marriage?: 'Let us be. . . as well bred as if we were not married at all'.

What is the man's response? Ibsen left Helmer inarticulate in his chair. 'Empty. She is gone.' What follows in Congreve is a discourse as long, articulate, and witty from the future husband, which proves Mirabell to be Millamant's equal in intelligence and good humour. The last speech of Millamant, because of the way it is going, implies and demands a response, which Congreve then gives. Especially the husband emphasizes the role of the wife as the mother of their children, and insists on marital sexual fidelity.

But there is no one definite, translatable 'message' which we may extract from the play situation here, any more than in Ibsen. The moral is built out of a tension of forces: the co-operation and opposition of man and woman generally; the nature of Mirabell and Millament specifically, viewed as if real people; the nature of the comic stage itself on which ideas are the subject of brilliant discourse which are in free play not subject to everyday restraints; the limitation of this kind of action to before marriage, with the expectation of happy marriage as the dramatic resolution, so that dramatic convention, and our sense of 'real' life (whatever that is) are in constant interplay. It cannot be pinned down and re-expressed as few useful conceptions to be carried away in one's pocket like cough sweets: in a moral dilemma suck one or two as needful. What one is seeking to understand is process, movement, interchange, something as mobile as the very processes of Millamant's speech and thought themselves.

Yet, at certain times, in certain works of theatre (as in all art) there comes a sense of revealed truth. The union of word and image, the resolution of the forces of the tale that has been told, come to focus in a moment which distils the very essence of life experience more memorably, more fully, more intensely even than life itself. We are deeply moved, and that moment may return again and again to speak to us. The record that men and women have left behind them of how art has spoken to them tells so often of such experience that its force must be acknowledged, and for some, will be recognized. This chapter, and this little book as a whole, has emphasized the potentialities of theatre texts to mean many things. The thrust has been towards discussion. Does it mean this, or does it mean that? Turn it this way and we perceive one quality, turn it another and we see something else. Theatre is Protean. That is part of the excitement. It is proper and natural to enjoy the game. It is right to be sceptical before those who come telling us that they, and no other, possess revealed truth. And yet there remain those moments when it is said, 'Yes, I recognize that. What has been said and done there is true. And that truth moves me profoundly.' This is so, it it not? But I cannot conclude this chapter by giving such an example. Such examples each of us finds alone, and yet the experience is part of the general experience of humanity.

Instead, consider the implications of the following passage from Tom Stoppard's *Rosencrantz and Guildenstern are Dead*. It is a work which explores what happens to those two characters in *Hamlet* when not directly involved in the action of that play. In one scene, as actors in *Hamlet*, they discuss with the leading Player from the touring troupe the nature of theatrical truth. In particular the conversation turns upon death. 'You die so many times', Guildenstern points out, 'how can you expect [the audience] to believe in your death?'. 'On the contrary', the Player replies 'it's the only kind they do believe. They're conditioned to it'.

I had an actor once who was condemned to hang for stealing a sheep – or a lamb, I forget which – so I got permission to have him hanged in the middle of a play. . . and you wouldn't believe it, he just *wasn't* convincing! It was impossible to suspend one's disbelief. . .

Is there no such thing as truth, but only such conventions as we accept as truth? Or is there something even beyond the convention itself? Guildenstern objects: 'You! – What do *you* know about *death*?' and the Player replies:

It's what the actors do best. They have to exploit whatever talent is given to them, and their talent is dying. They can die heroically, comically, ironically, slowly, suddenly, disgustingly, charmingly, or from a great height. My own talent is more general. I extract significance from melodrama, a significance which it does not in fact contain; but occasionally, from out of this matter, there escapes a thin beam of light that, seen at the right angle, can crack the shell of mortality.

(Act II)

Is that the truth?

6 Where Next?

It would be sensible, as the next step, to develop from small examples, taken out of context, to consideration of entire plays. A full discussion of the attitude to the Christian religion, for instance, shown in the extracts from *The Playboy of the Western World* or *The Jew of Malta* (their 'ideology') would demand an examination of the complete context. Likewise, a consideration of the function and the nature of the roles of Edmund (in *King Lear*) or Juno (in *Juno and the Paycock*) requires a knowledge of the whole work. Self-evidently such study is beyond the scope and intention of a brief introduction.

The absence of the entire play has denied the opportunity to follow through such matters as structural irony (in *King Oedipus* the audience know that the king has killed his father and married his mother, but he is ignorant), or dominant motif (the repetition of key words and concepts in different circumstances). In *King Lear*, for example, imagery of mental blindness (Lear cannot see the truth about his daughters) is picked up in physical action (Gloucester has his eyes put out). Likewise it has not been possible to follow any long sequence of dialogue to show how style and meaning change and inter-relate and how characters develop. Most basic of all, nothing has been said about *plot*. Plays tell stories, and the enjoyment of a good story is a fundamental human pleasure. Some of the methods of this introduction are more fully developed by the author in relation to entire plays – in the volume on *The Way of the World* in Edward Arnold's Studies in English Literature series (1981), and the chapter on *The Jew of Malta* in *Christopher Marlowe* (Leiden, E. J. Brill, 1981).

Several introductory books of theatre theory usefully supplement this short study. The closest in outlook and approach are Martin Esslin's *An Anatomy of Drama* (Abacus, 1978) which is practical in its outlook on theatrecraft, but does not offer substantial passages for discussion and Ronald Hayman's *How to Read a Play* (Methuen, 1977). J. L. Styan's *The Elements of Drama* (Cambridge, CUP, 1960) bases itself on specific examples, and the illustrations are numerous. It is therefore a long book. The approach is more that of the sensitive and intelligent literary critic than the active theatre man, and of the well-read critic too, for the range is wide and the reader is introduced to many plots. Esslin's and Styan's books would make an admirable complementary pair. Eric Bentley's *The Life of Drama* (Atheneum, Philadelphia, 1964) could be read next. His approach is concerned with the psychology of theatre, and is provocative, bursting with ideas, and overflowing with good humour.

Theory without knowledge cannot be tested. In addition to reading (and seeing) as many plays as possible, it is important to develop the historical sense. For what kind of stage was a play written? What was the nature of the company? How did a play like this fit into the repertory of the time? What was the relation of the theatre of the age to the specific audience, and to society in general? The *Revels History of Drama in English* (8 vols., Methuen, 1975–83) is the most recent series which the student might take as a point of departure. Since everyone reads Shakespeare, special mention must be made of Glynne Wickham's *Early English Stages* (Routledge, 1959–). It combines massive scholarship with direct practical experience of theatre. The reader who is prepared to make the substantial effort necessary to come to terms with it will not only have learnt a great deal about Shakespeare's stage, but also how to use evidence: what is the difference between fact and speculation.

The necessary absence of history from this theoretical introduction has led to certain major omissions. They are matters which the student should pursue further at the appropriate time. In the chapter on 'the empty space' nothing was said of the Restoration stage (after 1660) which occupies an intermediate position between the platform stage for which Shakespeare wrote, and the proscenium arch 'naturalism' of the late nineteenth century. Painted scenery had been introduced within the proscenium arch by the time of the Restoration, but actors normally performed in front of the arch. It suggests a varied (ambivalent) attitude to illusion and reality, particularly in comedies of intrigue and disguise, but it is a problematical matter not pursued by example here.

More advanced students will have noticed also that the word 'naturalism' has been given its popular meaning in this introduction: 'as if real' and that I have avoided the technical use of the terms 'naturalism' and 'realism' as they are sometimes used to refer to specific theories of theatre. I think the popular use is right, and the technical usage confusing. Esslin's discussion of technical vocabulary is useful later, however, and should be considered as a student's studies develop.

Another major omission is, quite simply, Ben Jonson – the father of English comic theatre and Shakespeare's great antithesis in that art. It would be difficult, however, to choose an example from Jonson without explaining something of his theories of theatre, and thus to distract from the experiential and experimental approach of this book by setting in the foreground a specific writer's interpretation of his craft. The true enthusiast for English theatre must read some Jonson (*The Alchemist* and *Volpone* are his most popular works), and by reading Jonson redress the imbalance created by the overexposure of Shakespeare, who in some ways is untypical of his times. On a more theoretical level, one should learn something of Jonson's concept of 'humours' and his distinction between the strong development of one particular trait in a character (the true humour) and the affectation of claiming a humour one does not possess. In the example from *The Way of the World* Congreve's development of Millamant's role is probably shaped by such Jonsonian ideas – in particular the interplay between her affectation of a chattering coquette, and her true, and disturbing, sexual love for Mirabell. So too, in any discussion of comic plot, Jonson's skill in manipulating and shaping events (and Jonson's models for so doing) would provide constant illustration and points of reference.

As the sense of history develops, a problem (and stimulus) arises. What is the relation between the archaeological restoration (as far as possible) of the original nature of the dramatic piece, and the potentialities of performance now? There is no classic tradition in British theatre such as one finds, for instance, in the Japanese Noh where the techniques of intonation and dance are handed down from one generation to the next, sometimes through the same family, so that the performer is taught the right way to do things, because that is the way things are done. On the contrary, on the British stage, the tradition of playing Shakespeare has been continually to adapt the text for new kinds of theatre space, new acting styles, new critical and directorial interpretations. *A Midsummer Night's Dream* has been performed in a gymnasium with the actors swinging from trapezes. The interpretation of Shakespeare through the ages might be taken as a mirror of the kind of theatre, criticism and society which has produced him, and not as a mirror of Shakespeare at all, who has disappeared into infinite plurality.

This introduction has continually stressed the potentiality of all texts to respond to varied readings and to suggest ways of performance rather than one invariable, simple and right meaning. It may be that this approach has in itself been conditioned by the 'Shakespeare experience'. The openness of Shakespeare to multiple readings has encouraged that kind of approach to theatre generally. A word of qualification at this point may not go amiss. Not all texts are equally open, nor are all traditions of performance, even within British theatre, as fluid as the Shakespearian. The idea that 'anything goes' is manifest nonsense. Some playwrights control the conditions of performance of their texts far more specifically than others – particularly in the late nineteenth century and onwards by elaborate descriptions of character and action. To break with that control is often to swim against the tide – to create a sense of major dislocation which may be interesting because it is new, but is substituting the craft of the critic or director for that of the writer, and effectively rewriting. There is all the difference in the world between a range of potential, and anarchy.

In this respect it would be useful once more for the student to read Ben Jonson, and, in comedy at least, match Shakespeare text for text, because Jonson does not write with the same openness as Shakespeare, and the roles, plot, ideas, action are so carefully integrated that to dislocate the part explodes the whole. In *The Merchant of Venice* it is possible to conceive Shylock as a tragic figure and still hold a production together in counterpoint of attitudes and response. It is not possible, I think, to do the same with Sir Epicure Mammon in *The Alchemist*. Ridicule and laughter are directed at him. He is not the cause of sympathetic weeping.

Beware then of too much Shakespeare. One should recognize, too, I suggest, that one of the conditions of potentiality is that it has limits.

To the sense of the history of what has been done in the past, one should add too an awareness of what is happening now, and learn to re-evaluate the past in the light of the present. It is not within the scope of this study to review the processes by which in our own century naturalism yielded to 'symbolism', 'expressionism', or 'absurdism', or the development of the politically committed 'epic theatre'. The correct understanding of such technical terms can only follow the direct acquisition of the knowledge of such writing. None the less certain works of theory may properly be related to this introduction. Peter Brook's *The Empty Space* (Penguin, 1972) is an admirably clear and brief account, by a practising craftsman, of a number of the main developments in thinking about the nature of theatre this century. Two of the great originals should at some time be approached directly: Stanislavski and Brecht. Stanislavski's name is particularly associated with the deeply felt, developed-from-within style of naturalistic playing. He helped create one of the most famous theatres of the modern world: the Moscow Art Theatre, and was intimately related to the development of Chekhov's work. That story is told in his *My Life in Art* (Geoffrey Bles, 1924) which is, for the literary critic, probably a more useful approach than his several treatises on acting or direction. Brecht is Stanislavski's great antithesis. He emphasizes the artificial nature of the stage, rather than its apparent naturalism; he asked of the audience intellectual appraisal of the social causes and consequences of action rather than empathy with individual entities. His theories are now collected (pub. by Methuen). A word of warning: his plays do not always, it is claimed by some, support the theories. (A useful general anthology is Eric Bentley's *The Theory of the Modern Stage*, Penguin, 1968.)

Finally, one must recognize that theatre is an envolving and ever-changing art, and is all around one. It is not just a literary study for the classroom. Theatre has developed into the cinema. It is in the sitting-room every night on the television. Some playwrights, like Pinter, write for both stage and screen. Some, like Dennis Potter, write only for television. One cannot isolate *now* (tonight's television) from *then* (a popular play at Shakespeare's Globe), nor one medium totally from another. It is appropriate to compare Eisenstein's *Ivan the Terrible* with *King Lear*, the work of Satayajit Ray with that of Chekhov. The boundaries of literacy have expanded.

These matters take us beyond the modest purposes of this introduction, and pedagogic instruction of this general nature is not the method. Let us return for one last occasion to a text and endeavour to summarize in one example – the longest – matters taken up in earlier chapters which may now (possibly) be brought together. The passage is from the last scene of *The Winter's Tale.*The play had begun as tragedy. King Leontes, jealous of his wife (Hermione), and of his friend (Polixenes), had caused the death of his wife and child (so he believed). Half way through the play the action has changed from tragedy to pastoral comedy – the crux being the famous stage direction: 'Exit, pursued by a bear' when Antigonus abandons the queen's baby daughter (and is eaten, off stage, by the bear). The child is reared by friendly shepherds and called Perdita (the lost girl). Now, as the scene begins, she has been re-united to her father and is betrothed to Polixenes's son. The queen's faithful serving woman (Paulina) now takes Leontes, Polixenes and the children to see a statue of the queen, which is kept 'lonely, apart'.

Paulina   . . . But here it is: prepare
                     To see the life as lively mock'd as ever
                     Still sleep mock'd death: behold! and say 'tis well.
                     [*She draws back a curtain and reveals a statue*]
                     I like your silence: it the more shows off
                     Your wonder; but yet speak: first you my liege.
                     Comes it not something near?

Leontes   Her natural posture!
                     Chide me, dear stone, that I may say indeed
                     Thou art Hermione; or rather, thou art she
                     In thy not chiding, for she was as tender
                     As infancy and grace. But yet, Paulina,
                     Hermione was not so much wrinkled; nothing
                     So aged as this seems.

Polixenes   O! not by much.

Paulina   So much the more our carver's excellence;
                     Which lets go by some sixteen years and makes her
                     As she liv'd now.

Leontes   As now she might have done,
                     So much to my good comfort, as it is

Now piercing to my soul. O! thus she stood,
Ever with such life of majesty, – warm life,
As now it coldly stands, – when first I woo'd her.
I am asham'd: does not the stone rebuke me
For being more stone than it? O, royal piece!
There's magic in thy majesty, which has
My evils conjur'd to remembrance, and
From thy admiring daughter took the spirits,
Standing like stone with thee.

Perdita   And give me leave,
And do not say 'tis superstition, that
I kneel and then implore her blessing. Lady,
Dear queen, that ended when I but began,
Give me that hand of yours to kiss.

Paulina   O patience!
The statute is but newly fix'd, the colour's
Not dry. . .

Leontes   Do not draw the curtain

Paulina No longer shall you gaze on't, lest you fancy
May think anon it moves.

Leontes   Let be, let be!
Would I were dead, but that, methinks, already –
What was he that did make it? See, my lord,
Would you not deem it breath'd, and that those veins
Did verily bear blood?

Polixenes   Masterly done:
The very life seems warm upon her lip.

Leontes The fixture of her eye has motion in't,
As we are mock'd with art.

Paulina   I'll draw the curtain;
My lord's almost so far transported that
He'll think anon it lives.

Leontes   O sweet Paulina!
Make me to think so twenty years together:
Not settled senses of the world can match
The pleasure of that madness. Let's alone.

Paulina I am sorry, sir, I have thus far stirr'd you: but
I could afflict you further. . .
. . . I'll make the statue move indeed, descend,
And take you by the hand; but then you'll think, –

	Which I protest against, – I am assisted
	Be wicked powers.
Leontes	What you can make her do,
	I am content to look on: what to speak,
	I am content to hear; for 'tis as easy
	To make her speak as move.
Paulina	It is requir'd
	You do awake your faith. Then, all stand still;
	Or those that think it is unlawful business
	I am about, let them depart.
Leontes	Proceed:
	No foot shall stir.
Paulina	Music, awake her: strike!

'Tis time; descend; be stone no more: approach;
Strike all that look upon with marvel. Come;
Bequeath to death your numbness, for from him
Dear life redeems you. You perceive she stirs:
[Hermione, who has been living in secret for sixteen years, descends.]
Start not; her actions shall be holy as
You hear my spell is lawful: do not shun her
Until you see her die again, for then
You kill her double. Nay, present your hand:
When she was young you woo'd her; now in age
Is she become the suitor!
[Hermione embraces Leontes]

(V.iii. 18–109)

It was said by the great Indian film maker Ray that in ending a work he considered his masterpiece, he chose significant action, and silence, not words, to conclude the work, and to suggest the future. Does this scene from Shakespeare lend itself to analysis likewise in terms of its action and, more, in the blocks placed in the way of action, and in the silences? I suggest, as the first and essential topic for discussion in the scene, that attention be directed to the drawing of the curtain to reveal the statue, the attempts to approach and how they are frustrated, the nature of the frustrated actions (the kiss) and the resolution of the frustration when, at length, Hermione moves. Consider also the silence of Perdita – she who was lost, Hermione's daughter – in relation both to the words of her father (Leontes), and also to the greater silence of the seemingly breathing statue of her mother. What resemblance does this suggest? What significant pattern is established between fathers and children in the scene? And what, finally, is the function of the wordless harmony of music?

The generic question demands consideration. What kind of expectation do we bring to this scene in a play which began as tragedy, but has since, and abruptly, moved to pastoral comedy? The presumption is that we move on to a happy resolution; there is a wish (at least), an expectation (perhaps), that somehow that statue will come alive, that the wife be restored to the husband, as the daughter has come back to the father. But what kind of elements are blending: fairy tale? fertility myth? even pantomime perhaps? and should we forget the tragic preliminary to this scene, which is piercing to the soul of Leontes, an affliction to him that moves him to the point of tears? Can we analyse as separable strands a texture so complex in the weaving as this?

In what way can we discuss the characters within the action, and the role that they play? First, in a scene orchestrated through relationships such as this is, expressed part in words, part in silence, part by motion, part by stillness, how far is it meaningful to separate out the individual role from the function of the part in the scene? Granted that this orchestration is understood, in what other way might one think about the characters? Are they, in some measure, alien creatures of the stage and of the world of fairy tale, myth, romance – whatever term seems appropriate to describe the extraordinary actions – distant from us like beings of another world seen as if in a dream acting out some hieratic or mythic ritual the meaning of which is so profound and mystic that words alone cannot communicate it? Significant act, the harmonies of music, the formal groupings of actors upon a stage – these things, more than words, tell us of the mystery which we see and hear. Or should one lay one's emphasis more upon the fundamental human relationships common to all mankind: father and child, husband and wife, youth and age, renewal and death, hope and grief, repentance and sin? (And what is the function of Paulina?) Yet, too, behind the scene, lies all the story of the play, all the action in which each character has been involved, and the words draw our attention to matters such as Leontes's memories of the last 16 years, the joy that he once had in his wife, the very fact that the statue itself has the wrinkles of time upon it. This is general nature, but it is also specific to these people in this situation in this plot in this play. Do we wrong the specific thisness of Shakespeare's writing, his ability to create individuals as well as types, exact events as well as general truths, if we refrain from asking what does Leontes feel that he weeps, Perdita that she is struck to stone, and above all, what does Hermione feel (for she is really alive) while she stands and waits until she is restored to life and to Leontes? How is this related to the flux and reflux of the verse dialogue? Again, what kind of subtle and flexible critical discourse do we need if we are to encompass all this?

Finally, what does it mean? On one level, perhaps, the old (trite, if we will) moral message of love and forgiveness. How bald the statement seems compared with the representation. It is there, but only within the world of fiction that the playwright has created. Something more complex than the simple statement is present. Consider again the action of the drawing of the curtain to reveal the statue, and the threat to conceal it again behind that curtain. That showing – is it not in some measure like the art of the theatre itself? Leontes says

. . . The fixture of her eye has motion in't,
As we are mock'd with art.

The text draws attention specifically to the nature of artistic allusion. It is the same issue Stoppard raises in the passage with which the previous chapter ended. In what way does art imitate life? It is the question of *mimesis* – an issue as old as art itself. It is inseparable from our understanding of the moral of this comedy, fairy tale, myth, piece of theatrecraft, and is a matter the action and the text requires one to reflect upon as much as on the issues of love and forgiveness, life and death. Consider the statue which we see. It is presented as a work of art – a resemblance of Hermione. It becomes as if magically alive, and then, we learn, 'naturally' Hermione herself who has lived retired for 16 years awaiting this day. But that is not naturalistic, in the sense of corresponding to everyday reality. Nor is this really Hermione, but an actor personating the character. Yet it is deeply moving, and moves us because we recognize a truth within the fiction, as if the theatre represented the world itself. Or is it, as was suggested by the motto of the Globe itself, that the whole world is a theatre?

Index